AGAINST LOVE

AGAINST LOVE

A POLEMIC

Laura Kipnis

Pantheon Books, New York

All rights reserved under International and Pan-American
Copyright Conventions. Published in the United States by
Pantheon Books, a division of Random House, Inc.,
New York, and simultaneously in Canada by
Random House of Canada Limited, Toronto.

Pantheon Books and colophon are registered trademarks
of Random House, Inc.

Portions previously appeared in *Critical Inquiry, Harper's,*
and *The New York Times Magazine.*

Library of Congress Cataloging-in-Publication Data

Kipnis, Laura.
Against love : a polemic / Laura Kipnis.
p. cm.
Includes bibliographical references.
ISBN 0-375-42189-0
1. Adultery.   I. Title

HQ806.K48 2003   306.73'6—dc21   2003042022

www.pantheonbooks.com

Book design by M. Kristen Bearse

Printed in the United States of America
First Edition
2 4 6 8 9 7 5 3 1

To the only begetter

—Shakespeare, *Sonnets*

CONTENTS

AGAINST LOVE

READER ADVISORY

Please fasten your seatbelts: we are about to encounter contradictions. The subject is love, and things may get bumpy.

To begin with, who would dream of being against love? No one. Love is, as everyone knows, a mysterious and all-controlling force, with vast power over our thoughts and life decisions. Love is boss, and a demanding one too: it demands our loyalty. We, in turn, freely comply—or as freely as the average subject in thrall to an all-powerful master, as freely as indentured servants. It's a new form of mass conscription: meaning it's out of the question to be summoned by love, issued your marching orders, and then decline to pledge body and being to the cause. There's no way of being against love precisely because we moderns are constituted as beings yearning to be filled, craving connection, needing to adore and be adored, because love is vital plasma and everything else in the world just tap water. We prostrate ourselves at love's portals, anxious for entry, like social strivers waiting at the ropeline outside some exclusive club hoping to gain admission to its plushy chambers, thereby confirming our essential worth and making us interesting to ourselves.

But is there also something a bit worrisome about all this uniformity of opinion? Is this the one subject about which no disagreement will be entertained, about which one truth alone is permissible? (Even cynics and anti-romantics: obviously true believers to the hilt.) Consider that the most powerful organized religions produce the occasional heretic; every ideology has its apostates; even sacred cows find their butchers. Except for love.

Hence the necessity for a polemic against it. Polemics exist to poke holes in cultural pieties and turn received wisdom on its head, even about sacrosanct subjects like love. A polemic is designed to be the prose equivalent of a small explosive device placed under your E-Z-Boy lounger. It won't injure you (well not severely); it's just supposed to shake things up and rattle a few convictions. Be advised: polemics aren't measured; they don't tell "both sides of the story." They overstate the case. They toss out provocations and occasionally mockery, usually because they're arguing against something so unquestionable and deeply entrenched it's the only way to make even a dent in the usual story. Modern love may be a company town—it may even come with company housing (also known as "domesticity")—but are we such social marionettes that we automatically buy all usual stories, no questions asked?

Please note that "against" is also a word with more than one meaning. Polemics aren't necessarily unconflicted (nor are the polemicists); rhetoric and sentiment aren't always identical twins. Thus, please read on in a conflicted and contradictory spirit. Such is the nature of our subject.

PROLOGUE

(or, *"Something Just Happened to Me."*)

"Would you like to dance?" You've mustered all the studied casualness you can, momentarily convincing yourself (self-deception is not entirely unknown in moments such as these) that your motives are as pure as the gold of your wedding band, your virtue as eternal as your mortgage payment schedule. This small act of daring accomplished, your body now pressed nervously against this *person* who's been casting winsome glances in your direction all night, you slowly become aware of a muffled but not completely unfamiliar feeling stirring deep within, a distant rumbling getting louder and louder, like a herd of elephants massing on the bushveld . . . oh God, it's your *libido,* once a well-known freedom fighter, now a sorry, shriveled thing, from swaggering outlaw to model citizen, Janis Joplin to Barry Manilow in just a few short decades. All rampant primal urges having long been successfully sublimated into job and family life, all applicable organs pledged to the couple as community property (and now very occasionally summoned to perform those increasingly predictable conjugal interchanges, but with—let's face it—somewhat flagging ardor, a gradually drooping interest), you suddenly recall with a thud just what you've been missing. When did sex get to be so boring? When did it turn into this thing you're

supposed to "work at"? Embarrassing isn't it, how long you can go without it if you don't remember to have it, and how much more inviting a good night's sleep can seem compared to those over-rehearsed acts. Even though it used to be pretty good—if memory serves—before there was all that sarcasm. Or disappointment. Or children. Or *history*.

The rest of the crowd is flailing around wildly with the graceless pseudo-abandon of responsible citizens on holiday furlough, in the vicinity of free liquor and eager to reassure themselves that they can still get down, no matter how terrible they're going to feel the next morning. (Maybe academics at an annual conference, thankful to be momentarily released from whining students and the life of the mind—but the profession doesn't matter, this could be anyone's story.) So here you are, bopping to the beat (you hope), awash in an exotic sensation. Is it . . . pleasure? A long time since someone looked at you with that kind of interest, isn't it? Various bodily and mental parts are stirred to attention by this close encounter with an anatomy not your mate's—who was dissuaded from coming, or wasn't interested in the first place, and . . .

Quash that thought, quickly. That is, if you can call what's going through your mind *thinking*.

Maybe it wasn't a party. Maybe it was an airplane, or your health club, or—for those who prefer living exclusively in the present—work. (Think hard: numerous awkward encounters for years to come.) The venue doesn't matter; what does is finding yourself so voluptuously hurtled into a state of possibility, a destabilizing, might-be-the-start-of-something kind of moment. You felt transformed: suddenly so charming, so attractive, awakened from emotional deadness, and dumbstruck with all the stabbing desire you thought you'd long outgrown. Then there was that first nervous phone call, coffee, or a drink, or—circumstances permitting—an incredible all-night marathon conversation. It's been so long since someone really *listened* to you like that. And laughed at your jokes, and looked wistfully into your eyes. And fascinated you. So long since you fascinated yourself. When you touch, "accidentally," an ache of longing lodges itself in mind and groin, replacing an emptiness you hadn't quite acknowledged was there. (Or had become accustomed to self-medicating with all the usual palliatives: martinis to Prozac.) Somehow things quickly get a little more serious than you'd anticipated, which you secretly (all right, desperately) wanted, and now *emotions* are involved, vulnerabilities are involved—emotions you didn't intend to have, vulnerability that thrills you to the core, and you shouldn't be feeling any of this, but also you're strangely . . . is it elated?

Hard on the heels of that elation is a combustible fusion of numbing anxiety and gnawing guilt. You seem to be sweating constantly, an unpleasant, clammy sweat. And Christ, is that a cold sore? Your stomach's going haywire; your conscience feels like an inflamed appendix, paining you, about to burst open with toxins and blame. A strange virus seems to have invaded your normally high-functioning immune system, penetrating your defenses, leaving you vulnerable, trembly, strangely flushed. It seems you've contracted a life-threatening case of desire. (The life it threatens is the one you've been leading, which now seems painfully lacking in a vital ingredient—a lack whose portrait now haunts every waking thought.)

Are you really the kind of person who *does* this sort of thing? It's all quite in advance of the fact, this self-torment, because you haven't really "done anything" yet, but you hate yourself anyway. You decide to talk it out with the new-found love-object—make the graceful exit. "I just can't," you explain mournfully, while realizing that, actually, you can. No reliable statistics are available on the average time lapse between utterances such as "I just can't" or "This probably isn't a good idea" and the commencement of fore-play, but sociolinguists should consider investigating their peculiar aphrodisiacal power. Anyway, guilt is a relief in its own way—it reassures you that you're really not a bad person. A bad person wouldn't be feeling guilty.

Or . . . maybe you've done this a few times before. Maybe even more than a few. Maybe you've made your own private bargain, periodically letting yourself off the fidelity hook in the small sense—keep it light, have some fun, don't mislead anyone—in order to maintain fidelity in the larger sense, upholding those long-ago commitments to the best of your abilities, despite everything. "Everything" here is shorthand for every trade-off you didn't intend to make or that well-thumbed catalogue of perceived injuries you carry with you at all times, or the mounting sexual rejections (each one a small but lasting wound to some deli-cate part of your being), or—fill in the blank yourself. And so far it's worked out (knock wood), no huge disasters (notwithstanding the occasional tense moment, a recrimi-nation here and there), because after all, you're fundamen-tally a decent person, honest in your fashion, and you don't mean to hurt anyone, and of course you love your partner, or at least can't imagine life apart (or the disruptions and

anguish and social ignominy such a breach would entail),
but you need—well, what you need isn't entirely the point,
and certainly not a discussion you intend to have with yourself (maybe after the kids are in college should there be kids,
if not just postponed to some indefinite point in the future)
because why open *that* can of worms, since once opened
those worms clearly aren't going to just crawl willingly
back into their can and the last thing you want is a big
wormy mess on your hands. Or for people to think you're
an asshole or a selfish bitch who doesn't care about anyone
but herself, or any of the other terms in which a threatened
community expresses moral opprobrium.

Whatever the specifics, here you are, poised on the threshold of a major commandment infraction, about to be inducted
(or perhaps reinstated, you devil) into the secret underground
guild of conjugal saboteurs, all recklessly clogging up the
social machinery with their errant desires. You have no clue
what you're doing, or what's going to come of it (situational
amnesia about the last time may be required), but you'd do
anything to keep on feeling so . . . *alive.*

And so . . . *experimental.* Adultery is to love-by-the-rules
what the test tube is to science: a container for experiments.
It's a way to have a hypothesis, to be improvisational: *"What
if . . . ?"* Or to take a conceptual risk. Like any experiment,
it might be a really bad idea or it might be a miracle cure—
transubstantiation or a potential explosion. Or both. Something new might be invented or understood: this could be
the next big paradigm shift waiting to happen. Or it could
just fizzle. But you never really know in advance, do you?

Chapter One

LOVE'S LABORS

Will all the adulterers in the room please stand up? This means all you cheating wives, philandering husbands, and straying domestic partners, past, present, and future. Those who find themselves fantasizing a lot, please rise also. So may those who have ever played supporting roles in the adultery melodrama: "other man," "other woman," suspicious spouse or marital detective *("I called your office at three and they said you'd left!"),* or least fun of all, the miserable cuckold or cuckoldess. Which, of course, you may be, without (at least, consciously) knowing that you are. Feel free to take a second to mull this over, or to make a quick call: *"Hi hon, just checking in!"*

It will soon become clear to infidelity cognoscenti that we're not talking about your one-night stands here: not about those transient out-of-town encounters, those half-remembered drunken fumblings, those remaining enclaves of suburban swinging—or any of the other casual opportunities for bodies to collide in relatively impersonal ways in postmodern America. We live in sexually interesting times, meaning a culture which manages to be simultaneously hypersexualized and to retain its Puritan underpinnings, in precisely equal proportions. Estimates of the percentage of those coupled who have strayed at least once vary from 20 to 70 percent, meaning that you can basically select any statistic you like to support whatever position you prefer to take on the prevalence of such acts. Whatever the precise number—and really, must we join the social scientists and pen-protector brigades and fetishize numbers?—apparently, taking an occasional walk on the wild side while still wholeheartedly pledged to a monogamous relationship isn't an earthshaking contradiction. Many of us manage to summon merciful self-explanations as required ("Shouldn't drink on an empty stomach") or have learned over the years to deploy the strategic exception ("Out-of-town doesn't count," "Oral sex doesn't count") with hairsplitting acumen. Perhaps a few foresightful types have even made prior arrangements with the partner to cover such eventualities—the "one time rule," the "must-confess-all rule" (though such arrangements are said to be more frequent these days among our non-heterosexual denominations). Once again, statistics on such matters are spotty.*

---

*Sexual self-reporting is notoriously unreliable. Consider the statistical problems plaguing the 1994 survey on sexual behavior by the University of Chicago National Opinion Research Center. Though touted as the most authoritative and thorough sex survey ever conducted, there was a small problem with the data: 64 percent of male sexual contacts reported couldn't be accounted for—or rather, they could if, in a pool of 3,500 responses, ten different women had each had 2,000 partners they didn't report. Sociologist Martina Morris, writing in the journal *Nature,* proposed a solution: eliminate the answers of male respondents who reported more than twenty partners in their lifetime or more than five in the previous year, which would make the numbers come out right. Leaving aside the question of whether men over-report more than women under-report sexual activity, or whether accumulating more than twenty partners in a lifetime defies probability, we might ask, does tweaking the

But we're not talking about "arrangements" with either self or spouse, or when it's "just sex," or no big thing. We will be talking about what feels like a big thing: the love affair. Affairs of the heart. Exchanges of intimacy, reawakened passion, confessions, idealization, and declarations— along with favorite books, childhood stories, relationship complaints, and deepest selves, often requiring agonized consultation with close friends or professional listeners at outrageous hourly rates because one or both parties are married or committed to someone else, thus all this merging and ardor takes place in nervous hard-won secrecy and is turning your world upside down. In other words, we will be talking about *contradictions,* large, festering contradictions at the epicenter of love in our time. Infidelity will serve as our entry point to this teeming world of ambivalence and anxiety, and as our lens on the contemporary ethos of love—as much an imaginary space as an actual event. (Commitment's dark other, after all—its dialectical pal.) Meaning whether or not you signed up for the gala cruise, we're all in this boat one way or another—if only by virtue of vowing not to be.

So just as a thought experiment—though it will never happen to *you* and certainly never has—please imagine finding yourself in the contradictory position of having elected to live a life from which you now plot intricate and

---

data on the basis of such assumptions make statistics any more reliable than guesses? As it happens, the Chicago survey reported quite low adultery rates (men 21 percent, women 11 percent), figures which are still widely quoted in current news stories on adultery. By comparison, the Kinsey reports pegged male adultery at 50 percent (in 1948) and female adultery (in 1953) at 26 percent.

meticulous escapes: a subdivision getaway artist, a Houdini of the homefront. You didn't plan it, yet . . . somehow here you are, buffeted by conflicting emotions, and the domesticity you once so earnestly pledged to uphold now a tailor-made straitjacket whose secret combination is the ingenious (and hopefully undetectable) excuses you concoct to explain your mounting absences (or mounting phone bills for you long-distance strayers; thank God for those prepaid phone cards, an adulterer's telephonic godsend). When defenses are down, or some minor domestic irritant unaccountably becomes an epic dispute—which happens even in the best of times, not only when you're preoccupied by thoughts of where you'd rather be and with whom—or when the yearning becomes physically painful, or you're spending an inordinate amount of time sobbing in the bathroom, this turn of events may raise fundamental questions about what sort of emotional world you want to inhabit, or what fulfillments you're entitled to, or—for a daring few—even the nerve-rattling possibility of actually *changing your life*. (Alternatively, forego hard questions and just up the Prozac dosage, which will probably take care of that resurgent libido problem too.)

A note on terminology: while adultery traditionally requires the prior condition of a state-issued marriage license for at least one of the parties, for the purposes of the ensuing discussion any coupled relationship based on the assumption of sexual fidelity will count as "married." And with gay populations now demanding official entry to state-sanctioned nuptials too, no longer is this the heterosexual plight alone: welcome aboard all commitment-seeking queer, bi, and transgendered compatriots. But gay or straight, licensed or not, anywhere the commitment to monogamy reigns, adultery provides its structural transgression—sexual exclusivity being the cornerstone of modern coupledom, or such is the premise—and for the record, you can also commit it with any sex or gender your psyche can manage to organize its desires around; this may not always be the same one that shapes your public commitments.

An additional terminological point. As our focus will be on "social norms" and "mainstream conventions" of love rather than exceptions and anomalies (and on the interesting penchant for inventing conventions that simultaneously induce the desire for flight), for the purposes of discussion terms like "love" and "coupledom," or "coupled" and "married," will often be used interchangably. Though coupledom is not always the sole outcome of romantic love, nor does love necessarily persist throughout coupledom's duration; though not all couples have joined into legal marriage contracts with the state; though a few iconoclasts do manage to love to the beat of a different drummer, let's agree at the outset that the sequence "love-couple-marriage" does structure prevailing social expectations, regardless of variations in individual practices. Feel free to make whatever semantic adjustments are required should some idiosyncrasy (or prolonged adolescent rebellion or bad luck streak or terminal ambivalence) on your part necessitate a different terminology. "Domestic partners," "significant others," even you "commitment-phobes": keep reading. There are a million stories in love's majestic empire, and yours is in here too.

And while we're clarifying terms, a note on gender. These days either partner can play either gender role, masculine or feminine, regardless of sex or sexual orientation. Thus, gender will not be a significant aspect of our discussion. Whoever waits at home, whoever "has their suspicions," is the wife. Whoever "wants more freedom" is the guy. And if the married-male/single-female configuration is still the most prevalent adultery form, all indications are that female straying is on the rise: clearly all that was required were more opportunities for women to get out of the house. (And more academic degrees: sociologists report that the higher a woman's education level, the more likely she is to have affairs; when the female partner has more education than the male, she's the one more likely to stray.) While feminism typically gets the credit (or blame) for propelling women out of the domicile and into the job market, let's give credit where credit is due: thanks must go too to economic down-turns and stagnating real wages—although if it now takes two incomes to support a household, maybe this was not exactly what the term "women's liberation" was designed to mean.*

---

*It remains to be seen whether feminism's greatest accomplishment was the liberation of women or whether it was redistributing feminine sub-mission more equally between the genders: this question will hover in the background of our discussion. Note that gender equity isn't necessarily synonymous with greater freedom; it can simply mean equality in sub-mission. The wave of civil and constitutional reforms that took place throughout the liberal democracies during much of the twentieth century did grant women equal status as legal subjects and did reform marital property laws; the questions being posed here will take up less evident forms of subjection, which intersect variously with gender reforms.

And, finally, a note on genre. This *is* a polemic. If there is scant attention paid to the delights of coupled fidelity and the rewards of long-term intimacies or the marvelousness of love itself, please remember that the polemicist's job is not to retell the usual story, and that one is well rehearsed enough that it should not need rehearsing once more here. Should its absence cause anxiety, if frequent bouts of sputtering are occluding your reading experience, just append where necessary.

Adulterers: you may now be seated. Will all those in Good Relationships please stand? Thank you, feel free to leave if this is not your story—you for whom long-term coupledom is a source of optimism and renewal, not emotional anesthesia. Though before anyone rushes for the exits, a point of clarification: a "good relationship" would probably include having—and wanting to have—sex with your spouse or spouse-equivalent on something more than a quarterly basis. (Maybe with some variation in choreography?) It would mean inhabiting an emotional realm in which monogamy isn't giving something up (your "freedom," in the vernacular) because such cost-benefit calculations just don't compute. It would mean a domestic sphere in which faithfulness wasn't preemptively secured through routine interrogations *("Who was that on the phone, dear?"),* surveillance *("Do you think I didn't notice how much time you spent talking to X at the reception?"),* or impromptu search and seizure. A "happy" state of monogamy would be defined as a state you don't have to *work* at maintaining. After all, doesn't the demand for fidelity beyond the duration of desire *feel* like work—or work as currently configured for so many of us handmaidens to the global economy: alienated, routinized, deadening, and not something you would choose to do if you actually had a choice in the matter?

Yes, we all know that Good Marriages Take Work: we've been well tutored in the catechism of labor-intensive intimacy. Work, work, work: given all the heavy lifting required, what's the difference between work and "after work" again? Work/home, office/bedroom: are you ever *not* on the clock? Good relationships may take work, but unfortunately, when it comes to love, trying is always trying too hard: work doesn't work. Erotically speaking, play is what works. Or as psychoanalyst Adam Phillips puts it: "In our erotic life . . . it is no more possible to work at a relationship than it is to will an erection or arrange to have a dream. In fact when you are working at it you know it has gone wrong, that something is already missing."

Yet here we are, toiling away. Somehow—how exactly did this happen?—the work ethic has managed to brown-nose its way into all spheres of human existence. No more play—*or* playing around—even when off the clock. Of course, the work ethic long ago penetrated the leisure sphere; leisure, once a respite from labor, now takes quite a lot of work itself. (Think about it the next time you find yourself repetitively lifting heavy pieces of metal after work: in other words, "working out.") Being wedded to the work ethic is not exactly a new story; this strain runs deep in middle-class culture: think about it the next time you're lying awake contemplating any of those 4 A.M. raison d'être questions about your self-worth or social value. (*"What have I* *really accomplished?")** But when did the rhetoric of the factory become the default language of love—and does this mean that collective bargaining should now replace marriage counseling when negotiating for improved domestic conditions?

When monogamy becomes labor, when desire is organized contractually, with accounts kept and fidelity extracted like labor from employees, with marriage a domestic factory policed by means of rigid shop-floor discipline designed to keep the wives and husbands and domestic partners of the world choke-chained to the status quo machinery—is this really what we mean by a "good relationship"?

Back in the old days, social brooders like Freud liked to imagine that there was a certain basic lack of fit between our deepest instincts and society's requirements of us, which might have left us all a little neurosis-prone, but at least guaranteed some occasional resistance to the more stifling demands of socialization. But in the old days, work itself occasionally provided motives for resistance: the struggle over wages and conditions of course, and even the length of the workday itself. Labor and capital may have eventually struck a temporary truce at the eight-hour day, but look around: it's an advance crumbling as we speak. Givebacks

---

*Note that sociologists have devised a somewhat ironical term for non-working populations—the unemployed, the welfare classes, the elderly, or criminals—presumably meant to reflect how they're seen by society. The term is "social garbage."

are the name of the game, and not just on the job either: with the demands of labor-intensive intimacy and "working on your relationship," now it's double-shifting for everyone.*
Or should we just call it vertical integration: the same compulsory overtime and capricious directives, the dress codes and attitude assessments, those dreaded annual performance reviews—and don't forget "achieving orgasm."

But recall that back in the old days the promise of technological progress was actually supposed to be *less* work rather than more. Now that's an antiquated concept, gone the way of dodo birds and trade unionism. How can you not admire a system so effective at swallowing all alternatives to itself that it can make something as abject as "working for love" sound admirable? Punching in, punching out; trying to wrest love from the bosses when not busily toiling in the mine shafts of domesticity—or is it the other way around? It should come as no surprise, as work sociologist Arlie Russell Hochschild reports, that one of the main reasons for the creeping expansion of the official workday is that a large segment of the labor force put in those many extra hours because they're avoiding going home. (Apparently domestic life has become such a chore that staying at the office is more relaxing.)

So when does domestic overwork qualify as a labor viola-

---

*But which sphere models the other? Recent United Nations statistics show employed Americans working an average of 49½ hours a week, and that's just at paid labor. This is an average of 3½ weeks a year more than Japanese workers (the previous world leaders), 6½ weeks more than British workers, and 12½ weeks more than German workers. Said the economist who compiled the report, "It has a lot to do with the American psyche, with American culture."

tion and where do you file the forms? For guidance on such questions, shall we go straight to the horse's mouth? This, of course, would be Marx, industrial society's *poète maudit,* so little read yet so vastly reviled, who started so much trouble so long ago by asking a very innocent question: "What is a working day?" For this is the simple query at the heart of *Capital* (which took three volumes to answer). As we see, Marx's question remains our own to this day: just how long should we have to work before we get to quit and goof around, and still get a living wage? Or more to our point, if private life in post-industrialism means that relationships now take work too, if love is the latest form of alienated labor, would rereading *Capital* as a marriage manual be the most appropriate response?

What people seem to forget about Marx (too busy blaming him for all those annoying revolutions) is how evocatively he writes about *feelings.* Like the feeling of overwork. The motif of workers being bled dry keeps cropping up in his funny, mordant prose, punctuated by flurries of over-the-top Gothic metaphors about menacing deadness. The workday is a veritable graveyard, menaced by gruesome creatures and ghouls from the world of the ambulatory dead; overwork produces "stunted monsters," the machinery is a big congealed mass of dead labor, bosses are "bloodsucking vampires," so ravenous to extract more work from the employees to feed their endless werewolf-like hunger for profit, that if no one fought about the length of the workday it would just go on and on, leaving us crippled monstrosities in the process, with more and more alienated labor demanded from our tapped-out bodies until we dropped dead just from exhaustion.

Funny, the metaphors of the homefront seem to have acquired a rather funereal ring these days too: *dead* marriages, *mechanical* sex, *cold* husbands, and *frigid* wives, all going through the motions and keeping up appearances. Your desire may have withered long ago, you may yearn—in inchoate, stumbling ways—for "something else," but you're indentured nevertheless. *Nothing must change.* Why? Because you've poured so much of yourself into the machinery already—your lifeblood, your history—which paradoxically imbues it with magical powers. Thus will social institutions (factories in *Capital,* but love is a social institution too) come to subsume and dominate their creators, who don't see it happening, or what they've lost, or that the thing they themselves invented and bestowed with life has taken them over like a hostile alien force, like it had a life of its own. Or so Marx diagnosed the situation at the advent of industrialism.

A doleful question lingers, and with no answer yet in sight: *Why work so hard?* Because there's no other choice? But maybe there is. After all, technological progress could reduce necessary labor to a minimum had this ever been made a social goal—if the goal of progress were freeing us from necessity instead of making a select few marvelously rich while the luckless rest toil away. Obviously the more work anyone has to do, the less gratification it yields—no doubt true even when "working on your relationship"—whereas, being freed from work would (to say the least!) alter the entire structure of human existence, not to mention jettison all those mildewed work-ethic relationship credos too—into the dustbin of history they go. "Free time and you free people," as the old labor slogan used to go. Of course, free people might pose social dangers. Who knows what mischief they'd get up? What other demands would come next?

As Marx should have said, if he didn't: "Why work when you can play? Or play around?" (Of course, playing around sometimes gets to be serious business too; about which, more to come.) Historical footnote: Marx was quite the adulterer himself.

Whining about working conditions won't make you too popular with management though, so keep your complaints to yourself. Obviously the well-publicized desperation of single life—early death for men; statistical improbability of ever finding mates for women—is forever wielded against reform-minded discontented couple-members, much as the grimness of the USSR once was against anyone misguided enough to argue for systematic social reforms in a political argument (or rash enough to point out that the "choices" presented by the liberal democracies are something less than an actual choice). *"Hey, if you don't like it here, just see how you like it over there."* Obviously, couple economies too are governed—like our economic system itself—by scarcity, threat, and internalized prohibitions, held in place by those incessant assurances that there are "no viable alternatives." (What an effective way of preventing anyone from thinking one up.) Let's note in passing that the citizenship-as-marriage analogy has been a recurring theme in liberal-democratic political theory for the last couple of hundred years or so, from Rousseau on: these may feel like entirely personal questions, but perhaps they're also not without a political dimension? (More on this to come.)

How we love and how we work can hardly be separate questions: we're social creatures after all—despite all those enlightening studies of sexual behavior in bonobos and red-winged blackbirds claiming to offer important insights into the nuances of human coupling. Harkening back to some remote evolutionary past for social explanations does seem to be a smoke screen for other agendas, usually to tout the "naturalness" of capitalist greed or the "naturalness" of traditional gender roles. Man as killer ape; woman as nurturing turtledove, or name your own bestial ancestor as circumstance requires. (When sociobiologists start shitting in their backyards with dinner guests in the vicinity, maybe their arguments about innateness over culture will start seeming more persuasive.) No, we're social creatures to a fault, and apparently such malleable ones that our very desires manage to keep lockstep with whatever particular social expectations of love prevail at the moment. What else would explain a polity so happily reconciled to social dictates that sex and labor could come to function like one inseparable unit of social machinery? Where's the protest? Where's the outrage? So effectively weeded out—and in the course of just a few short generations too—that social criticism is now as extraneous as a vestigial organ. Note that the rebellion of desire against social constrictions was once a favorite cultural theme, pulsing through so many of our literary classics—consider *Romeo and Juliet* or *Anna Karenina*. Now apparently we've got that small problem solved and can all love the way that's best for society: busy worker bees and docile nesters all.

Despite the guise of nature and inevitability that attaches itself to these current arrangements, the injunction to work at love is rather a recent cultural dictate, and though the vast majority of the world's inhabitants may organize themselves into permanent and semi-permanent arrangements of two, even the most cursory cross-cultural glance reveals that the particulars of these arrangements vary greatly. In our own day and part of the globe, they take the form of what historians of private life have labeled the "companionate couple," voluntary associations based (at least in principle) on intimacy, mutuality, and equality; falling in love as the prerequisite to a lifelong commitment that unfolds in conditions of shared domesticity, the expectation of mutual sexual fulfillment. And by the way, you will have sex with this person and this person alone for the rest of eternity (at least in principle).

The odd thing is that such overwhelming cultural uniformity is also so endlessly touted as the triumph of freedom and individuality over the shackling social conventions of the past (and as if the distinctly regulatory aspect of these arrangements didn't cancel out all such emancipatory claims in advance). Equally rickety is the alternate view that these arrangements somehow derive from natural law—love as an eternal and unchanging essence which finds its supreme realization in our contemporary approach to experiencing it. The history of love is written differently by every historian who tackles the subject; without becoming mired in their internecine debates, we can still say with certainty that nothing in the historical or the anthropological record indicates that our amorous predecessors were "working on their relationships." Nor until relatively recently was marriage the expected venue for Eros or romantic love, nor was the presumptive object of romantic love your own husband or wife (more likely someone else's), nor did anyone expect it to endure a lifetime: when practiced, it tended to be practiced episodically and largely outside the domicile.

But our focus here is not historical, so let's stick to modern love and its claims. Freedom over shackling social conventions—really? If love has power over us, what a sweepingly effective form of power this proves to be, with every modern psyche equally subject to its caprices, all of us allied in fearsome agreement that a mind somehow unsusceptible to love's new conditions is one requiring professional ministrations. Has any despot's rule ever so successfully infiltrated every crevice of a population's being, into its movements and gestures, penetrated its very soul? In fact it creates the modern notion of a soul—one which experiences itself as empty without love. Saying "no" to love isn't just heresy, it's tragedy: for our sort the failure to achieve what is most essentially human. And not just tragic, but abnormal. (Of course the concept of normalcy itself is one of the more powerful social management tools devised to date.) The diagnosis? It can only be that dread modern ailment, "fear of intimacy." Extensive treatment will be required, and possibly social quarantine to protect the others from contamination.

If without love we're losers and our lives bereft, how susceptible we'll also be to any social program promoted in its name. And not only the work ethic: take a moment to consider domestic coupledom itself. What a feat of social engineering to shoehorn an entire citizenry (minus the occasional straggler) into such uniform household arrangements, all because everyone knows that true love demands it and that any reluctance to participate signals an insufficiency of love. What a startling degree of conformity is so meekly accepted—and so desired!—by a species, *homo Americanus,* for whom other threats to individuality do so often become fighting matters, a people whose jokes (and humor is nothing if not an act of cultural self-definition) so frequently mock others for their behavioral uniformity—communism for its apparatchiks, lemmings for their skills as brainless followers—yet somehow fails to notice its own regimentation in matters at least as defining as toeing a party line, and frequently no more mindful than diving off high cliffs en masse.

Of course love may have its way with us, but it's also a historical truism that no form of power is so absolute that it completely quashes every pocket of resistance. We may prostrate ourselves to love—and thus to domestic coupledom, modern love's mandatory barracks—but it's not as though protest movements don't exist. (If you're willing to look in the right places.) Regard those furtive breakaway factions periodically staging dangerous escape missions, scaling barbed-wire fences and tunneling for miles with sharpened spoons just to emancipate themselves—even temporarily.

Yes, *adulterers:* playing around, breaking vows, causing havoc. Or . . . maybe not just playing around? After all, if adultery is a de facto referendum on the sustainability of monogamy—and it would be difficult to argue that it's not—this also makes it the nearest thing to a popular uprising against the regimes of contemporary coupledom. But let's consider this from a wider angle than the personal dimension alone. After all, social theorists and political philosophers have often occupied themselves with similar questions: the possibilities of liberty in an administered society, the social meaning of obligation, the genealogy of morality—even the status of the phrase "I do" as a performative utterance, a mainstay question of the branch of philosophy known as speech act theory. Might we entertain the possibility that posing philosophical questions isn't restricted to university campuses and learned tomes, that maybe it's something everyone does in the course of everyday life—if not always in an entirely knowing fashion? If adultery is more of a critical practice than a critical theory, well, acting out *is* what happens when knowledge or consciousness about something is foreclosed. Actually, that's what acting out is for. Why such knowledge is foreclosed is a question yet to be considered—though how much do any of us know about our desires and motivations, or the contexts that produce them? We can be pretty clueless. We say things like "Something just happened to me," as if it were an explanation.

Social historians assessing the shape of societies past often do look to examples of bad behavior and acting out, to heretics, rebels, criminals—or question who receives those designations—because ruptures in the social fabric also map a society's structuring contradictions, exposing the prevailing systems of power and hierarchy and the weak links in social institutions. If adultery is a special brand of heresy in the church of modern love, clearly it's a repository for other social contradictions and ruptures as well.* This isn't to say that adultery is a new story—it's hardly that. It does mean that it's a story that gets reshaped by every era as required. Ours, for instance, made it into the basis for an extended period of national political scandal— this after decades, if not centuries, of relative inattention to the matter. And after previously handing politicians carte blanche to stray with impunity, suddenly yanking back the privilege. Why?

One consequence (if not a cause) was the opportunity it created for exiled questions about the governing codes of intimate life—including how well or badly individuals negotiate them—to enter the national political discussion. Clearly there's pervasive dissatisfaction with the state of marriage: the implosion rate is high and climbing. Equally clearly, the reasons for that dissatisfaction is a discussion that can't publicly take place. Understandably: consider the network of social institutions teetering precariously on companionate love's rickety foundations—which means, frankly, that large chunks of contemporary social existence are built on the silt of unconsciousness, including large sectors of the economy itself. Given the declining success story of long-term marriages, as reported in the latest census, we're faced with a social institution in transition, and no one knows where it's going to land. The reasonable response would be to factor these transitions into relevant policy and social

---

*Of course, heretics also invariably fascinate—entire Inquisitions are devoted to probing their views. (See Carlo Ginzburg's *The Cheese and the Worms*, an ingenious case study of one medieval heretic and the fascination he exerted over his inquisitors.)

welfare decisions; this is apparently impossible. Instead, we're treated to a parade of elected representatives moralizing in public and acting out their own marital dissatisfactions in private, as if the entire subject had been exiled to the outer boroughs of unconsciousness—there to be performed à deux for the citizenry by naked politicians pantomiming the issues like players in some new avant garde form of national political dinner theater. But given the levels of confusion (and disavowal) surrounding these questions, is it so surprising that they just keep popping up unbidden into public view like a chronic rash or an unsightly nervous condition? Or surprising that they'd be channeled into scandal, the social ritual of choice for exposing open secrets (and for ritually shaming anyone they can be pinned to, thus exempting the rest of us and temporarily healing the rupture)? Scandal is the perfect package for circulating such dilemmas. More on this to come.

To recap. Among the difficult (and important) questions our adulterer-philosophers and roving politicians have put before us is this: Just how much renunciation of desire does society demand of us versus the degree of gratification it provides? The adulterer's position—following a venerable tradition of radical social theory—would be: *"Too much."* Or this: Is it the persistence of the work ethic that ties us to the companionate couple and its workaday regimes, or is it the ethos of companionate coupledom that ties us to souldeadening work regimes? On this one the jury is still out.

Adultery is not, of course, minus its own contradictions. Foremost among them: What are these domestic refuseniks and matrimonial escape artists escaping *to,* with such determination and cunning? Well, it appears that they're escaping to . . . *love.* As should be clear, ours is a story with a significant degree of unconsciousness, and not a little internal incoherence. (Or as Laura puts it to Alec in *Brief Encounter,* the classic infidelity story: "I love you with all my heart and soul. I want to die.")

Thus, please read on in a tolerant spirit.

If adultery is the sit-down strike of the love-takes-work ethic, regard the assortment of company goons standing by to crush any dissent before it even happens. (Recall too the fate of labor actions past, as when the National Guard was ordered to fire on striking workers to convince them how great their jobs were, in case there were any doubts.) Needless to say, any social program based on something as bleak as working for love will also require an efficient enforcement wing to ply its dismal message. These days we call it "therapy." Yes, we weary ambivalent huddled masses of discontent will frequently be found scraping for happier consciousness in the discreetly soundproofed precincts of therapy, a newly arisen service industry owing its pricey existence to the cheery idea that ambivalence is a curable condition, that "growth" means adjustment to prevailing conditions, and that rebellion is neurotic—though thankfully, curable.

But no rest for the weary when you're in therapy! Resenting the boss? Feeling overworked or bored or dissatisfied? Getting complaints about your attitude? Whether it's "on the relationship" or "on the job," get yourself right to the therapist's office, pronto. The good news is that there are only two possible diagnoses for all such modern ailments (as all we therapy-savants know): it's going to be either "intimacy issues" or "authority issues." The bad news is that you'll soon discover that the disease doubles as the prescription at this clinic: you're just going to have to "work harder on yourself." If a nation gets the leaders it deserves, can the same be said for its therapies?

Of course according to Freud—arguably a better theorist than therapist himself (he could get a little pushy with the patients)—desire *is* regressive, and antisocial, and *there's no cure,* which is what makes it the wild card in our little human drama. (And also so much fun.) It screws up all well-ordered plans and lives, and to be alive is to be fundamentally split, fundamentally ambivalent, and unreconciled to the trade-offs of what Freud called, just a bit mockingly, "civilized sexual morality."* But Freud was long ago consigned to conformist therapy's historical ash can, collectively pilloried for his crimes against decency and empiricism (Philip Wylie: "Unfortunately, Americans, who are the most prissy people on earth, have been unable to benefit from Freud's wisdom because they can *prove* that they do not, by and large, sleep with their mothers"). So don't sign up for therapy if you're looking for radical social insights—or social insights at all actually: what's for sale here is "self-

---

*And was Freud an adulterer? It seems unlikely, though one of his would-be debunkers, a rather singular historian of psychoanalysis named Peter Swales, has made it his life's work (these debunkers are a zealous bunch) to prove that Freud and his sister-in-law Minna Bernays were an item.

knowledge." (Only a cynic could suspect it of being remedial socialization in party clothes.) As you will soon discover under the tutelage of your kindly therapist, all those excess desires have their roots in some childhood deprivation or trauma, which has led to lack of self-esteem or some other impeded development which has made you unable to achieve proper intimacy and thus prone to searching for it in all the wrong places, namely anywhere outside the home. (You can be fairly certain it's not going to be those social norms that need a tune up; sorry, hon—it's you.) Conflicts in the realm of desire act out something "unresolved" in the self, a deeply buried trove of childhood memories or injuries that you will spend years excavating, in regular office visits and at no small cost. But don't resist! The more you resist the longer it takes, and the more you'll pay—in forty-five-minute increments, and at fees far exceeding the median daily wage. But happily, you will soon be feeling far better about yourself, and at peace with your desires and conflicts; if not, the same results can be attained in easy-to-swallow capsule form. With an estimated thirty million Americans— or around 10 percent of the adult population—having ingested antidepressants to date (GPs apparently hand them out like lollipops), better living through chemistry is now the favored social solution. Just say goodbye to your sex life.*

Another of the company goons: Culture. Consider the blaringly omnipresent propaganda beaming into our psy-

---

*Harvard psychiatrist Joseph Glenmullen, author of *Prozac Backlash,* estimates that up to 60 percent of those who take Prozac or other SSRIs (the most widely prescribed category of antidepressants) experience drug-induced sexual dysfunction as a side effect.

ches on an hourly basis: the millions of images of lovestruck couples looming over us from movie screens, televisions, billboards, magazines, incessantly strong-arming us onboard the love train. Every available two-dimensional surface touts love. So deeply internalized is our obedience to this capricious despot that artists create passionate odes to its cruelty; audiences seem never to tire of the most repetitive and deeply unoriginal mass spectacles devoted to rehearsing the litany of its torments, forking over hard-earned dollars to gaze enraptured at the most blatantly propagandistic celebrations of its power, fixating all hopes on the narrowest glimmer of its fleeting satisfactions. But if pledging oneself to love is the human spirit triumphal, or human nature, or consummately "normal," why does it require such vast PR expenditures? Why so much importuning of the population?

Could there be something about contemporary coupled life itself that requires all this hectoring, from the faux morality of the work ethic to the incantations of therapists and counselors to the inducements of the entertainment industries, just to keep a truculent citizenry immobilized within it? Absent the sell tactics, would the chickens soon fly the coop, at least once those initial surges of longing and desire wear off? (Or more accurately, flap off in even greater numbers than the current 50 percent or so that do?) As we know, "mature love," that magical elixir, is supposed to kick in when desire flags, but could that be the problem right there? Mature love: it's kind of like denture adhesive. Yes, it's supposed to hold things in place; yes, it's awkward for everyone when it doesn't; but unfortunately there are some things that glue just won't glue, no matter how much you apply.

Clearly the couple form as currently practiced is an ambivalent one—indeed, a form in decline say those census-takers—and is there any great mystery why? On the one hand, the yearning for intimacy, on the other, the desire for autonomy; on the one hand, the comfort and security of routine, on the other, its soul-deadening predictability; on the one side, the pleasure of being deeply known (and deeply knowing another person), on the other, the strait-jacketed roles that such familiarity predicates—the shtick of couple interactions; the repetition of the arguments; the boredom and the rigidities which aren't about to be transcended in this or any other lifetime, and which harden into those all-too-familiar couple routines: the Stop Trying To Change Me routine and the Stop Blaming Me For Your Unhappiness routine. (Novelist Vince Passaro: "It is difficult to imagine a modern middle-class marriage not syncopated by rage.") Not to mention the *regression,* because, after all, you've chosen your parent (or their opposite), or worse, you've become your parent, tormenting (or withdrawing from) the mate as the same-or-opposite-sex parent once did, replaying scenes you were once subjected to yourself as a helpless child—or some other variety of family repetition that will keep those therapists guessing for years. Given everything, a success rate of 50 percent seems about right (assuming that success means longevity).

Or here's another way to tell the story of modern love. Let's imagine that to achieve consensus and continuity, any society is required to produce the kinds of character structures and personality types it needs to achieve its objective—to perpetuate itself—molding a populace's desires to suit particular social purposes. Those purposes would not be particularly transparent to the characters in question, to those who live out the consequent emotional forms as their truest and most deeply felt selves. (That would be us.)

Take the modern consumer. (Just a random example.) Clearly, routing desire into consumption would be necessary to sustain a consumer society—a citizenry who fucked in lieu of shopping would soon bring the entire economy grinding to a standstill. Or better still, take the modern depressive. What a boon to both the pharmaceutical and the social-harmony industries such a social type would be. These are merely hypotheticals, of course, since it's not as if we live in a society of consumers and depressives, or as if the best therapy for the latter weren't widely held to be strategically indulging in the activities of the former— "retail therapy" in urban parlance.

But perhaps there would be social benefits to cultivating a degree of emotional stagnation in the populace? Certain advantages to social personality types who gulped down disappointment like big daily doses of Valium, who were so threatened by the possibility of change that the anarchy of desire was forever tamed and a commitment to perfect social harmony effortlessly achieved? Advantages to a citizenry of busy utilitarians, toiling away, working harder, with all larger social questions (is this *really* as good as it gets?) pushed aside or shamed, since it's not like you have anything to say about it anyway.

Some of our gloomier thinkers have argued that there is indeed a functional fit between such social purposes and modes of inner life, a line of thinking associated with the generation of social theorists known as the Frankfurt School, who witnessed the rise of fascism in Germany first-hand and started connecting the dots between authoritarian personality types, the family forms that produced them, and the political outcomes. In fact, according to renegade psychoanalyst Wilhelm Reich, a Frankfurt School fellow traveler, the only social purpose of compulsory marriage for life is to produce the submissive personality types that mass society requires. He also took the view—along with Freud—that suppressing sexual curiosity leads to general intellectual atrophy, including the loss of any power to rebel. (Not a point destined to attract large numbers of adherents, since, if true, the consequent intellectual atrophy would presumably prevent recognition of the condition.) A variation on the argument has it that social forms—economic forms too—arise on the basis of the personality types already in place. Capitalism itself clearly requires certain character structures to sustain it, and would never have gotten off the ground, according to early sociologist Max Weber, if it weren't for the prep work of religious asceticism. Capitalism only succeeded, says Weber, because it happened along at the heyday of Calvinism, already busy churning out personalities so steeped in sacrifice that the capitalist work ethic wasn't a difficult sell.* Personality types will continue to be tweaked as necessary: once consumer capitalism arrived it required an overlay of

---

*Weber, who coined the term "work ethic": yet another major adulterer. And one so transformed by his belated awakening to erotic experience, according to biographers, that it propelled the direction of his later (some say best) work on the conflicts between eroticism or other varieties of mystical religiosity and the processes of rationality. (Yes, adultery's eternal dilemma.)

hedonism on top of the productivity, at least to the extent that hedonism can be channeled into consumption. Witness the results: a society of happy shopaholics for whom shopping is not just a favored form of recreation, it's an identity.

Though when it comes to repression, perhaps we also come equipped with a secret talent for it? So intimated Freud, its most savvy chronicler. A certain degree of basic repression is necessary for any civilization to survive: if we were all just humping each other freely whenever the impulse arose, what energy would be left for erecting a culture? But with civilization achieved and now on firm enough footing, do we push it further than necessary, churning out *surplus repression,* in the phrase of another Frankfurt fellow traveler, Herbert Marcuse? Could we be a little nervous about the possibility of our own freedom? Consider how little resistance those repressive forces meet as they ooze their way into the neighborhoods of daily life. Resistance? More like mademoiselles greeting the occupying fascist troops with flirtatious glances and coy inviting smiles. *"What cute jackboots, monsieur."* Basking in their warm welcome from a docile populace, those repressive tendencies, now completely emboldened, reemerge unfettered in the guise of social character types, marching in goose step to the particular requirements of the day: the "professional," the "disciplinarian," the "boss," the "efficiency expert." Observe such types—your friends and neighbors—toiling away at work and home, each accompanied by an internal commanding officer (the collaborationist within) issuing a steady string of silent directives. "Will-power!" "Grow up!" "Be realistic!" "Get busy!" "Don't play around!" And thus we become psyches for whom repression has its own seductions. How *virtuous* it feels, trading play for industry, freedom for authority, and any lingering errant desires for "mature" realizations like Good Relationships Take Work.

Us, rebel? More like trained poodles prancing on hind legs, yipping for approval and doggie treats. So exiled have even basic questions of freedom become from the political vocabulary that they sound musty and ridiculous, and vulnerable to the ultimate badge of shame—"That's so '60s!"—the entire decade having been mocked so effectively that social protest seems outlandish and "so last-century," just another style excess like love beads and Nehru jackets. No, rebellion won't pose a problem for this social order. But just in case, any vestiges of freedom (or any tattered remnants still viable after childhood's brute socialization) will need to be checked at the door before entering the pleasure palace of domestic coupledom. Should you desire entry, that is. And who among us does not—because who can be against love?

But just for fun, try this quick thought experiment. Imagine the most efficient kind of social control possible. It wouldn't be a soldier on every corner—too expensive, too crass. Wouldn't the most elegant means of producing acquiescence be to somehow transplant those social controls so seamlessly into the guise of individual needs that the difference between them dissolved? And here we have the distinguishing political feature of the liberal democracies: their efficiency at turning out character types who identify so completely with society's agenda for them that they volunteer their very beings to the cause. But . . . *how* would such a feat be accomplished? *What* mysterious force or mind-altering substance could compel an entire population into such total social integration without them even noticing it happening, or uttering the tiniest peep of protest?

What if it could be accomplished through *love*? If love, that fathomless, many-splendored thing, that most mutable yet least escapable of all human experiences, that which leads the soul forward toward wisdom and beauty, were also the special potion through which renunciation could, paradoxically, be achieved? The paradox being that falling in love is the nearest most of us come to glimpsing utopia in our lifetimes (with sex and drugs as fallbacks), and harnessing our most utopian inclinations to the project of social control would be quite a singular achievement in the annals of modern population management. Like soma in *Brave New World*, it's the perfect drug. "Euphoric, narcotic, pleasantly hallucinant," as one character describes it. "All the advantages of Christianity and alcohol; none of their defects," quips another.

Powerful, mind-altering utopian substances do tend to be subject to social regulation in industrialized societies (as with sex and drugs): we like to worry about whether people will make wise use of these things. What if they impede productivity! So we make them scarce and shroud them in prohibitions, thus reinforcing their danger, along with the justification for social controls.

Clearly love is subject to just as much regulation as any powerful pleasure-inducing substance. Whether or not we fancy that we love as we please, free as the birds and butterflies, an endless quantity of social instruction exists to tell us what it is, and what to do with it, and how, and when. And tell us, and tell us: the quantity of advice on the subject of how to love properly is almost as infinite as the sanctioned forms it takes are limited. Love's proper denouement, matrimony, is also, of course, the social form regulated by the state, which refashions itself as benevolent pharmacist, doling out the addictive substance in licensed doses. (It could always be worse: the other junkies are forced to huddle outside neighborhood clinics in the cold for their little paper cups; love at least gets treated with a little pomp and ceremony.) Of course, no one is physically held down and forced to swallow vows, and not all those who love acquire the proper licenses to do so, but what a remarkable compliance rate is nevertheless achieved. Why bother to make marriage compulsory when informal compulsions work so well that even gays—once such paragons of unregulated sexuality, once so contemptuous of whitebread hetero lifestyles—are now demanding state regulation too? What about re-envisioning the form; rethinking the premises? What about just insisting that social resources and privileges not be allocated on the basis of marital status? No, let's *demand regulation!* (Not that it's particularly easy to re-envision anything when these intersections of love and acquiescence are the very backbone of the modern self, when every iota of self-worth and identity hinge on them, along with insurance benefits.)

So, here you are, gay or straight, guy or gal, with matrimony (or some functional equivalent) achieved, domestication complete, steadfastly pledged and declawed. A housetrained kitten. But wait: what's that nagging little voice at the edge of your well-being, the one that refuses to shut up, even when jabbed with the usual doses of shame. The one that says: *"Isn't there supposed to be something more?"* Well maybe there is, but don't go getting any "ideas," because an elaborate domestic security apparatus is on standby, ready to stomp the life out of them before they can breed—stomp them dead like the filthy homewrecking cockroaches they are.

Sure, we all understand jealousy. Aren't all precarious regimes inherently insecure, casting watchful eyes on their citizenry's fidelity, ready to spring into action should anything threaten the exclusivity of those bonds? Every regime also knows that good intelligence props up its rule, so it's best to figure you're always being watched—you never know exactly from where, but a file is being compiled. Like seasoned FBI agents, longtime partners learn to play both sides of the good cop/bad cop routine. *"Just tell me, I promise I'll understand. . . . You did WHAT?!"* Once suspicions are aroused, the crisis alarm starts shrilling, at which point any tactics are justified to ensure your loyalty. Since anything can arouse suspicion, "preventative domestic policing" will always be an option: loyalty tests, trick questions, psychological torture, and carefully placed body blows that leave no visible marks. (Private detectives are also an option, or if you like, a Manhattan company called Check-a-Mate will send out attractive sexual decoys to see if your mate will go for the bait, then issue a full report.)*

---

*Or consider the possibilities opened up by new technologies. A Web site called Adulteryandcheating.com counsels tactics like satellite tracking and cyber-spying to nab cheating partners; spy equipment stores are

Sure, easy to feel sympathetic to wronged partners: humiliated, undesired, getting fat, deserving better. The question of why someone cheats on you or leaves you can never be adequately explained. ("Intimacy issues," no doubt.) Realizing that people are talking, that friends knew and you didn't, that someone else has been poaching in your pasture and stealing what is by law yours *is* a special circle of hell. And even if you don't much want to have sex with the mate anymore, it's a little galling that someone else does. (Though this knowledge sometimes sparks a belated resurgence of desire: the suspicion-ridden marriage bed can be a pretty steamy place.)

But here's a question for you spouse-detectives as you're combing through credit card receipts, or cracking e-mail passwords, or perfecting the art of noiselessly lifting up phone extensions, counting condoms or checking the diaphragm case: What are you hoping to find? If you're looking, you basically know the answer, right? And if you don't find anything this time, are you willing to declare the matter settled? Hardly! Suspicion is addictive, sometimes even gratifying. After all, rectitude is on your side, and you want those promises kept, damn it. You want those vows *obeyed*. You want security, and of course you want love—since don't we all? But you'll settle for obedience, and when all else fails, ultimatums might work. But it's not as though you

---

also promoting new keystroke-capture programs as a surveillance system for suspicious spouses, which, once installed on a home computer, will record your partner's e-mail exchanges and Web site visits for your later review.

don't know when you're being lied to (though what constitutes "knowing" and "not knowing" in this regard could
fill another book) and having transformed yourself into a
one-person citizen-surveillance unit, how can you not hate
the mate for forcing you to act with such a lack of dignity?

Here we come to the weak link in the security-state model
of long-term coupledom: *desire.* It's ineradicable. It's roving
and inchoate, we're inherently desiring creatures, and sometimes desire just won't take no for an answer, particularly
when some beguiling and potentially available love-object
hoves into your sight lines, making you feel what you'd forgotten how to feel, which is *alive,* even though you're supposed to be channeling all such affective capacities into the
"appropriate" venues, and everything (Social Stability! The
National Fabric! Being a Good Person!) hinges on making
sure that you do. But renunciation chafes, particularly when
the quantities demanded begin to exceed the amount of
gratification achieved, for instance when basic monogamy
evolves, as it inevitably does under such conditions, into
surplus monogamy: enforced compliance rather than a free
expression of desire. (Or "repressive satisfaction" in Marcuse's still handy, still stinging phrase.) The problem is that
maybe we're really *not* such acquiescent worker bees in our
desires, and maybe there actually *isn't* consent about being
reduced to the means to an end, especially when the end is
an overused platitude about the social fabric, whatever that
is. Meaning what?—that we'll all just churn out the proper
emotions to uphold calcified social structures like cows produce milk, like machines spit out O-rings?

But start thinking like that, and who knows what can
happen? And that's the problem with dissatisfaction—it

gives people "ideas." Maybe even critical ideas. First a glimmering, then an urge, then a transient desire, soon a nascent thought: *"Maybe there's something else."* Recall that the whole bothersome business with labor unions and workers demanding things like shorter workdays started out the same way: a few troublemakers got fed up with being treated like machines, word spread, and pretty soon there was a whole movement. "Wanting more" is a step on the way to a political idea, or so say political theorists, and ideas can have a way of turning themselves into demands. In fact, "wanting more" is the simple basis of all utopian thinking, according to philosopher Ernst Bloch. "Philosophies of utopia begin at home," Bloch liked to say—found in the smallest sensations of pleasure and fun, or even in daydreams, exactly because they reject inhibitions and daily drudgery. Utopianism always manages to find an outlet too, operating in disguise when necessary, turning up in all sorts of far-flung places. Or right under our noses, because utopianism is an aspect of anything that opens up the possibilities for different ways of thinking about the world. For madcap utopian Bloch, the most tragic form of loss wasn't the loss of security, it was the loss of the capacity to imagine that things could be different.

And for us? If philosophies of utopia begin at home, if utopianism is buried deep in those small, lived epiphanies of pleasure, in sensations of desire, and fun, and play, in love, in transgression, in the rejection of drudgery and work, well . . . no one *works* at adultery, do they? If this makes it a personal lab experiment in reconfiguring the love-to-work ratio, or a makeshift overhaul of the gratification-to-renunciation social equation, then it's also a test run for the most verboten fly-in-the-ointment question of all: *"Could things be different?"* No, it may not be particularly thought-out, or even articulable, but what else is behind these furtive little fantasies and small acts of resistance—playing around, acting out, chasing inchoate desires and longings—but just trying to catch fleeting glimpses of what "something else" could feel like? (Not that anyone here is endorsing adultery! After all, it hardly needs endorsements, it's doing quite well on its own. New recruits are signing up by the minute.)

Sure, adulterers behave badly. Deception rules this land, self-deception included. Not knowing what you're doing risks bad faith, and living exclusively in the present, and leaving sodden emotional disasters strewn behind. But note the charges typically leveled against the adulterer: "immaturity" (failure to demonstrate the requisite degree of civilized repression); "selfishness" (failure to work for the collective good—a somewhat selectively imposed requirement in corporate America); "boorishness" (failure to achieve proper class behavior). Or the extra fillip of moral trumping: "People will get hurt!" (Though perhaps amputated desires hurt too.) True, typically in outbursts of mass dissatisfaction—strikes, rebellions, sedition, coups—people sometimes get hurt: beware of sharp rocks and flying debris. But if adultery summons all the shaming languages of bad citizenship, it also indicates the extent to which domestic coupledom is the boot camp for compliant citizenship, a training ground for gluey resignation and immobility. The partner plays drill sergeant and anything short of a full salute to existing conditions is an invitation to the stockades—or sometimes a dishonorable discharge.

Still, conflicted desires and divided loyalties don't present a pretty picture when seen up close: the broken promises, the free-range seductiveness, the emotional unreliability, all perched a little precariously on that chronic dissatisfaction, crashing up against the rocky shoals of desperation. Ambivalence, universal though it may be, isn't much fun for anyone. (Least of all when you're on the receiving end. Deceived partners everywhere: our sympathies.) Ambivalence may fade into resignation, and given a high enough tolerance for swallowing things, this is supposed to count as a happy ending. But ambivalence can also be another way of saying that we social citizens have a constitutive lack of skill at changing things. Understandably—who gets any training at this? Even when not entirely resigned to the social institutions we're handed, who has a clue how to remake them, and why commit to them if there could be something better? Unfortunately, "something better" is also an idea so derided it's virtually prohibited entry to consciousness, and consequently available primarily in dreamlike states: romantic love and private utopian experiments like adultery (or secondhand, in popular fantasy genres like romance and myth). But after all, we don't make history under conditions of our own choosing, and private life is pretty much all we have to work with when it comes to social experiments in our part of the world these days, where consumer durables and new technologies come equipped with planned obsolescence, and social institutions are as petrified as Mesozoic rock formations.

Still, before signing up for the thrill ride of adultery, a word to the wise. Let's all be aware that passionate love involves alarmingly high degrees of misrecognition in even the best of cases (that poignant Freudian paradigm), which means that we players in the adultery drama will be especially beset, madly flinging ourselves down uncharted paths in states of severe aporia, the impediments to self-knowledge joined at the hip to the lures of disavowal. All of us risk drowning in those swirling tidal waves of emotion and lust, cramped up and overwhelmed, having thought ourselves shrewd and agile enough to surf the crest despite the posted danger signs. You may say you're not going to get in too deep, you may say you just want to have fun, but before you know it you're flattened by a crashing wave from nowhere and left gasping for air with a mouthful of sand. (Translation: you're in love, or you're in lust, and not with your mate, and your life feels out of control, and maybe you've been waiting your whole life to feel this way about someone, which means you're in big trouble.)

So watch out, baby—a few missteps, a couple of late-night declarations, and everything could be up for grabs. What started as a fling has somehow turned serious; the supplement has started to supersede the thing that needed supplementing. Perhaps unplanned exposures have forced things into the open, or those "contradictions" of yours have started announcing themselves in some unpleasant somatic form that eventually can't be ignored. Insomnia. Migraines. Cold sores. Digestive ailments. Heart palpitations. Sexual difficulties. (Sometimes bodies just won't play along, even when instructed otherwise.) Choices will need to be made. Choices that you, with your terminal ambivalence and industrial-strength guilt, are not capable of making. Antacids aren't working. Work is suffering. The shrink just says, "What do you think?" But about what? Love is also a way of forgetting what the question is. Using love to escape love, groping for love outside the home to assuage the letdowns of love at home—it's kind of like smoking and wearing a nicotine patch at the same time: two delivery systems for an addictive chemical substance that feels vitally necessary to your well-being at the moment, even if likely to wreak unknown havoc in the deepest fibers of your being at some unspecified future date.

The best polemic against love would be too mimic in prose the erratic and overheated behavior of its hapless practitioners: the rushes and excesses, the inconsistent behavior and inchoate longings, the moment-by-moment vacillations between self-doubt *("What am I doing?")* and utter certainty *("You're the one")*, all in quest of something transformative and unknown. It would replicate in form the impediments and trade-offs and fumbling around, all the things felt but not understood, and the tension of being caught in-between—between mates and lovers or between rival ways of telling such conflicted tales, each beckoning with its own sultry and alluring vocabulary: social theory and love affairs, Marx and Freud, utopia and pragmatics, parody and sentimentality. "Just pick one and settle down already," you can hear people saying. But what if you just keep finding yourself looking "elsewhere" as much as you tell yourself not to, because this is really no way to act? Yes, just like all you adultery clowns out there tripping over your big floppy shoes and chasing improbable fulfillment, knowing it has the whiff of a doomed undertaking and making up the rules as you go along, we polemicists too are propelled to (intellectual) promiscuity, rashness and blind risks and becoming the neighborhood pariah (or joke) just for thinking there could be reasons to experiment with reimagining things.

But to those feeling a little stultified and contemplating a spin down Reinvention Road: do weigh your options carefully. Don't forget that all outbreaks of love outside sanctioned venues still invite derisive epitaphs like "cheating" or "mid-life crisis," while those that play by the rules will be community-sanctified with champagne and gifts in the expensive over-rehearsed costume rituals of the wedding-industrial complex (its participants stiffly garbed in the manner of landed gentry from some non-existent epoch: clearly, playing out unnatural roles is structured into these initiation rites as a test of the participants' stamina for role-playing as a social enterprise and as a measure of their resolve and ability to keep doing so in perpetuity).

Consider this not just a polemic, but also an elegy: an elegy for all the adultery clowns crying on the inside, with our private experiments and ragtag utopias. The elegiac mode traditionally allows a degree of immoderation, so please read on in an excessive and mournful spirit—or at least with some patience for the bad bargains and compensatory forms the discontented classes engineer for themselves in daily life. So many have met such dismal, joyless fates, dutifully renouncing all excess desires, and along with them any hopes that the world could deliver more than it currently does—or could if anyone had the temerity to fight about it, and face down the company goons, then face down the ritual shaming, and last but not least the massive self-inflicted guilt shortly to follow.

But beware their seductive and dangerous lures too, those beguiling adulterers, dangerous as pirate ships lying in wait to cadge any unguarded troves of emotion and pleasure, promises brandished like a swashbuckler's sword, slicing through qualms like they were air. Was ever there a more seductive seducer, or a more captivating captor, than an emotionally starving human with potential ardor in sight? *("Trust me, things will work out.")* But to all you temporary utopians and domestic escape artists who couldn't sustain your own wishes for more courageous selves or different futures or love on better terms, who could only filch a few brief moments of self-reinvention and fun before being drop-kicked, guilt-ridden and self-loathing, back to the domestic gulags, the compartmentalization, the slow death of "maturity" (because risking stagnation is obviously preferable to risking change in the prevailing emotional economy): we mourn your deaths. We leave big immoderate bouquets at your gravesides.

Chapter Two

DOMESTIC GULAGS

Adultery is one way of protesting the confines of coupled life; of course there's always murder. (Neither is necessarily proposed as a *solution*.) Given the regularity with which episodes of spousal mayhem hit the newsstands, evidently opting for homicide over the indignities of divorce court or the travails of marriage counseling not infrequently strikes overwrought wives, husbands, lovers, and exes as the only available solution to the frustrating impasses of together-ness and the emotional thickets of relationships. From those early heady heartthrob days (the little gifts, the silly phone calls) to the guns and ammo catalogue, from lover's lane to the state pen, from the optimism of two souls merging to the impossibility of basic communication: "intimate vio-lence" is such a regular occurrence that it merits its own sta-tistical category in the Bureau of Justice annual compilation of crime figures, which helpfully subcategorizes such forms of intimacy into "lethal" and "non-lethal" varieties.

No doubt we'd all prefer to think that such grisly fates always befall someone else. But logically speaking, *some-one* must eventually play the unlucky role of "someone else." Will it be you? Will it be me? Is it just possible that at this very moment something we've said or done, inadvertently—or maybe not (if there's one thing every partner knows it's just how to push the other person's buttons)—is driving our secretly unhinged mates to contemplate putting our bodies through a wood chipper, or stabbing us and the kids and blaming it on hippie marauders, or haplessly trying to outsource the job to FBI agents impersonating killers-for-hire? All true stories of Love Gone Wrong and Good Spouses Gone Bad—terribly bad. (Remember, they always appear normal right up until they snap, just ask the neighbors. *"He was always out in front washing the car. I never thought anything about it, but you know, now it seems kind of suspicious."*)

Indeed, what would fill true crime's allotted bookstore shelves if not for all the inventively murderous mates in our midst? Would true crime even exist as a genre if not for the evident cultural fascination with every last lurid detail of lethal love? Celebrity murders or those among the society set never fail to captivate and are, needless to say, headline staples—all the better if they contain some kinky elements, or at least improbable alibis. Recent example: the washed-up television actor charged with hiring his bodyguard to shoot his wife in the parking lot of a Studio City restaurant where they had just dined, the actor having momentarily dashed back into the restaurant to retrieve the handgun he said he'd left there. (Handgun? Couldn't it have been . . . a wallet?) Non-celeb and local stories provide their own appeals, like the opportunity for artful headlines. "Man's Stabbed; Wife's Nabbed"—a nice bit of headline poetry from the *New York Daily News*. Of the numerous non-celeb spousal killings, it's interesting to note which stories get picked up by the wire services, elevated from the local crime beat to national attention; these tend to be the ones with an ironic twist or quirky cast of characters, sometimes so resembling stand-up punch lines—"Kill my wife, please"— or shaggy dog stories, so full of guilty amusement that you have to remind yourself that someone actually died. (Spouse murder often seems to have an unaccountably jokey aspect to it, assuming it's not someone you know.) In Irving, Texas, a 530-pound woman deliberately killed her husband by sitting on him during an argument. In Washington, D.C., a best-selling romance writer was murdered by her lawyer-husband. (Who could read this without wondering if he was tall, dark, and handsome?) In New York, a rabbi was convicted of hiring a member of his own congregation to kill his wife; it was the killer rather than the spiritual leader who was overcome by conscience and confessed.

"Non-lethal intimate violence" also provides macabre fascinations. You have your mutilations—a usually submissive Virginia wife takes butcher knife in hand to sever hubby from a favorite body part. Your disfigurements—a bereft Queens boyfriend pays three men to throw lye in his girlfriend's face when she tries to break it off with him. (She, left scarred and partially blinded by the attack, agreed for reasons known best to herself to marry him after he emerged from prison fourteen years later; then stood by him when he was accused, some thirty-five years later at age seventy, of threatening to kill his forty-two-year-old mistress, who had recently ended their five-year affair.) Your attempted poisonings—this a method typically favored by wives, featuring antifreeze, weed killer, and oleander tea (beware if served: highly lethal). Even your poignant moments—this one courtesy of the *Ottawa Citizen:* "Man Says Hatchet Attack No Reason For Divorce." ("I still love her, I don't care. If she gets crazy and cuts my head off, I still love her. I'd take her back.") Your eviscerations—a certain former New York mayor announces his plans to divorce his wife, to the press corps prior to actually informing the wife herself. Unfortunately, the Justice Department does not compile statistics on emotional violence or subcriminal forms of non-lethal intimate behavior: verbal abuse, or public undermining, or emotional blackmail, or everyday manipulations (often involving children), or all the other varieties of less-than-stellar couple conduct in our midst.

Should love come packaged with health advisories: Caution, May Be Addictive As Well As Harmful to Your Ongoing Survival? (Or to your dignity or self-worth?) Should coupling be categorized as a high-risk activity if it regularly leads habitués to such extremes of antisocial behavior and creative acts of mayhem? Or if it increases the likelihood of you becoming their object? Sometimes there's no getting out clean either: uncoupling too can prove dangerous. Recall the famous Scarsdale diet doctor shot to death by his diet-pill-addled headmistress-girlfriend after he took up with his nurse; the San Diego society matron who murdered her ex and his new young bride in their sleep; a certain notorious ex–football hero turned movie star, turned acquitted murderer.

Cultural explanations for the pervasiveness of mate-brutalizing and aggression tend to have an inherently non-explanatory quality to them. The bad apple theory gets the most play, but the problem is that we're clearly talking about bushels, not a few stray worms. Those in quest of better reasons may turn to psychological explanations about the proximity of love and hate, or eros and aggression; some find feminist analyses about sanctioned male violence to women useful (except that even if women are typically the victims of intimate violence, men are not entirely immune: in 1998 some 160,000 men were reported victims of violent assault by an intimate partner). But consider another explanation: perhaps these social pathologies and aberrations of love are the necessary fallout from the social conventions of love that we all adhere to and live out on a daily basis. The more cynical version of this position would be that something about love is inherently impossible; the more optimistic one would be that just the conventions are inherently impossible. Nevertheless, recall that Freud did derive the general workings of the psyche from studying hysterics and neurotics; perhaps we too will come to understand more about the normal conditions of love through our inquiries into love gone wrong.

Let's begin with the fact that falling in love, in the current intimacy regime, doesn't just mean committing to another person, it means committing to certain emotional bargains and trade-offs also, some of which prove more workable than others. It's generally understood that falling in love means committing to *commitment*. This might seem obvious, but actually it isn't. Different social norms could entail something entirely different: yearly renewable contracts, for example. And if we weren't so emotionally yoked to the social forms we've inherited that trying to envision different ways of having a love life seems intellectually impossible and even absurd, who knows what other options might present themselves?

Despite our paeans to commitment, clearly it proves not an entirely salutary experience across the board. Take the pervasiveness of intimate violence. The problem here is hardly lack of commitment; this is commitment in overdrive: being less committed might mean being able to walk away. But these emotional bargains of ours do prove obdurate, and few of us manage to uncommit, when this proves necessary, without leaving big bloody clumps of self behind. Because in the current emotional regime, as we know, falling in love also commits us to *merging*. Meaning that unmerging, when this proves necessary, is ego-shattering and generally traumatic. The fear and pain of losing love is so crushing that most of us will do anything to prevent it, especially when it's not our choice. And since forestalling trauma is what egos are designed to do, with anxiety as an advance warning system (unfortunately a largely ineffective one), this will mean that falling in love also commits us to anxiety—typically externalized in charming behaviors like jealousy, insecurity, control issues (the list goes on)—or, in some cases, to externalized violence—the response of a system in emotional overload. The ego experiencing intimations of impending loss—real or imagined—is not a pretty sight.

Perhaps the problem begins, as Freud and followers have variously implied, with the gloomy fact that adult love doesn't ever completely quell that constitutional human sense of lack and separation trauma that sets its quest in motion. Anxiety is not just endemic to the enterprise, it's also incurable: however assiduously we devote ourselves to love's pursuit and conquest, the fretful specter of loss permeates the scene. Nevertheless, there we are, chasing tantalizing glimpses of some lost imaginary wholeness in a lover's adoring gaze, or in the "types" that we favor, or in the romantic scenarios we reenact or repeat. There we are, hop-

ing that the flimsy social safety nets we've committed ourselves to—monogamy, domesticity, maturity—resolve our
anxieties; that "security" or "commitment" (or children, or
real estate) are functional salves, even if the fetid quantities
of apprehension pooled just beneath the floorboards bode a
different story.

> From George Cukor's *The Marrying Kind:*
> Divorce court judge: Just what did you want out of
>   marriage?
> Florence: What I didn't get.

A society's lexicon of romantic pathologies invariably expresses its particular anxieties. High on our own list would
be diagnoses like "immaturity," or "inability to settle down,"
leveled at those who stray from our domestic-couple norms,
either by refusing entry in the first place, or pursuing various escape routes once installed: excess independence, ambivalence, "straying," divorce. For us modern lovers, *maturity*
is not a depressing badge of early senescence and impending decrepitude; for us maturity is a sterling achievement,
a sign of your worth as a person and your qualifications
to love and be loved. (Though isn't this "maturity" business a bit of an anti-aphrodisiac in itself?—won't those
geriatric years hobble along soon enough? Note that the
American Association of Retired Persons calls its monthly
publication *Modern Maturity*—just one more incentive to
aspire to this enviable state. Never too early to make a down
payment on those matching cemetery plots!) Clearly the
injunction to achieve "maturity"—loose translation: 30-year

mortgages, spreading waistlines, and shrunken libidos—finds its raison d'être in modern love's supreme anxiety, that structuring contradiction about the size of the San Andreas fault, upon which, unfortunately, the entirety of our emotional well-being rests, namely the expectation that romance and sexual attraction will persist throughout a lifetime of coupled togetherness, despite much hard evidence to the contrary.

Ever optimistic, heady with love's utopianism, most of us eventually pledge ourselves to unions that will, if successful, far outlast the desire that impelled them into being. The prevailing cultural wisdom is that even if sexual desire tends to be a short-lived phenomenon, nevertheless, that wonderful elixir "mature love" will kick in just in time to save the day, once desire flags. The question remaining unaddressed is whether cutting off other possibilities of romance and sexual attraction while there's still some dim chance of attaining them in favor of the more muted pleasures of "mature love" isn't similar to voluntarily amputating a healthy limb: a lot of anesthesia is required and the phantom pain never entirely abates. But if it behooves a society to convince its citizenry that wanting change means personal failure, starting over is shameful, or wanting more satisfaction than you have is illegitimate, clearly grisly acts of self-mutilation will be required.

Note that there hasn't always been quite such optimism about love's longevity, nor was the supposed fate of social stability tied to making it last beyond its given duration. For the Greeks, love was a disordering and thus preferably brief experience; the goal of marriage an orderly and well-managed household, not a path toward salvation or self-realization.

In the reign of courtly love, love was illicit and usually fatal. Passion meant suffering; the happy ending didn't yet exist in the cultural imagination. As for togetherness as an eternal ideal, the twelfth-century advice manual *De Amore et Amoris Remedio* (Treatise on Love and its Remedies) warned that too many opportunities to see or chat with the beloved would certainly decrease love. The innovation of happy love didn't even enter the vocabulary of romance until the seventeenth century; before the eighteenth century—when the family was primarily an economic unit instead of a hothouse of unmet needs—marriages were business alliances arranged between families and participants had little to say in the matter. (Passion was what you had *outside* marriage.) Wives were a form of property; wifely adultery was a breach of male property rights, and worse, it mucked up the orderly transmission of property via inheritance. It was only with the rise of the bourgeoisie—whose social power was no longer based on landholdings and inherited wealth—that marriages based on love rather than family alliances became the accepted practice. In other words, love matches became socially accepted once they no longer posed an economic threat to the class in power.

There are different ways to tell the story, and the historians all disagree, but it's evident from all accounts that our amatory predecessors didn't share our particular aspirations about their romantic lives—at least they didn't devote themselves to trying to sustain a fleeting experience past its shelf life or transform it into the basis of a long-term relationship. There may have been romantic torment, and the occasional intrepid romantic forerunner often paid the price—Heloise's lover, Peter Abelard: "They cut off those parts of my body with which I had committed the offense they deplored"—but the emphasis on love as a uniquely individual experience presupposes the existence of the modern individual. This is the one that comes equipped with specifically modern qualities like self-reflexiveness and psychological interiority: each one of us an embattled and unique personality, searching moors and countryside for that one beloved counterpart who will meet our unique psychological needs—conceptions of the self that, according to most historians, had little currency much before the late seventeenth century. In fact, a number of historians consider our version of romantic love a learned behavior that became fashionable only in the late eighteenth century, along with the new fashion for novel reading—the novel itself being a then-recent cultural form, invented precisely to explore all the hidden crevices of this newly burgeoning individuality. Other new cultural genres—autobiography, in particular—would figure here too. (Even archconservative Allan Bloom blames it all on Rousseau, who saw bourgeois love as a salve for the empty emotional center of restrained, lawbound societies and so elevated romance into a soul-saving experience.)

Fond as we are of projecting our own emotional quandaries backward through history, construing vivid costume dramas featuring medieval peasants or biblical courtesans tormented by our own longings and convoluted desires, sharing their feelings and dissecting their motives with the post-Freudian savvy of lifelong analysands, at least consider the fundamental social differences that provided the texture of premodern personal life: for instance, the near total absence of privacy prior to the eighteenth century (historian

Phillipe Ariès: "Until the end of the seventeenth century, nobody was ever left alone"), or the complete legal subordination of women to men. Then there's sex. As literary scholar Ruth Perry points out, another eighteenth century innovation was sexual disgust: when Charlotte Lucas marries the repellent Mr. Collins in *Pride and Prejudice* in a "pragmatic match" and talks it over afterward with her girlfriends, there's no hint that sharing the bed of an odious man might cause a girl feelings of disgust. The point is that sex didn't have the same psychological resonance as it does for the contemporary psyche: physical revulsion at sex with the wrong person was a learned and socially instituted response. More than that, it was an effective social management tool, since once internalized it institutes the psychology of monogamy as a self-enforced system. As Perry puts it: "If women were to stay put as the sexual property of one man and one man only, they had to be trained to feel repugnance for physical relations with anyone else"—which also suggests that the psychology of sex is more of a historical contingency than we're often inclined to consider.

But it may be that other things have changed less than we like to imagine. However much the decline of arranged marriages is held up in this part of the globe as a sign of progress and enlightenment (including, lately, as propaganda for modernity when seeking to score political points against Islam), however much it flatters our illusions of independence to imagine that we get to love whomever and however we please, this story starts to unravel if you look too closely. Economic rationality was hardly eliminated when individuals began choosing their own mates instead of leaving the job to parents; it plays as much of a role as ever. Despite all the putative freedom, the majority of us select partners re-markably similar to ourselves—economically, and in social standing, education, and race. That is, we choose "appro-priate" mates, and we precisely calculate their assets, with each party gauging just how well they can do on the open market, knowing exactly their own exchange value and that of prospective partners. (Exchange value includes your looks, of course. Look closely at newspaper engagement announcement photos—as social psychologists have in fact done and reported upon—and you will note that virtually every couple is quite precisely matched for degree of physi-cal attractiveness.) Scratch the romantic veneer, and we're hard-nosed realists armed with pocket calculators, calipers, and magnifying glasses. The real transformation of modern love, as sociologist Eva Iluouz points out, comes with the fact that ranking mates for material and social assets is now incorporated into the psychology of love and unconscious structures of desire, with individuals having now internal-ized the economic rationality once exerted by parents, thus "freely" falling in love with mates who are also—coinciden-tally—good investments. (Marrying down really isn't the norm, though certain assets are fungible categories—as we know, rich ugly men not infrequently nab beautiful women and vice versa.) Nevertheless, economic rationality in mate selection is now largely tacit in mainstream speech codes rather than the open matter it once was, and to ensure that it stays tacit we've devised a useful vocabulary of paralogical terms like "chemistry" and "clicking," as more descriptive terms like "economic self-interest" aren't considered polite. We do retain slightly dusty terms like "gold digger" or "fortune hunter" for those who jump rank or aren't subtle enough about their economic motives for current sensitivities. Terms like "good provider" or "security" may occasionally be invoked favorably in middle class culture, though their usage is strictly governed; discussing economic rationality in too much detail tends to be regarded as either déclassé or cold: it violates implicit personhood norms. (Speech codes may vary in different class strata or ethnic groups, but every social group has its codes and you breach them at the risk of exclusion.)

In other words, despite all the supposed freedom, the social rules governing mate selection are as finicky and precise as they were in Jane Austen's day. The difference is that it's now taboo to acknowledge them, which may amount to less freedom rather than more. What's now constrained isn't mate choice alone, it's any Austenesque acuity about the process. Falling in love itself is subject to the same bans on cognition: social protocols dictate that it be regarded as an elusive and slightly irrational procedure. Too much rationality or thinking risks killing the romance—and of course risks defying prevailing conceptions of the normal human: reptilian analogies like "cold-blooded" tend to be deployed against anyone displaying too much cognition where mooniness should prevail. But since falling in love *is* such a pleasure, and who wouldn't want to, clearly the only thing to do is to think as little as possible and hope for the best.

But even sans thinking, it's hard not to be aware that all is not so peachy in the land of love and romance. As love has increasingly become the center of all emotional expression in the modern imagination—the quantity without which life seems forlorn—anxiety about obtaining it in sufficient quantities and for sufficient duration has increased to the point that that anxiety suffuses the population, and most of our cultural forms. With the central premise of modern love the expectation that a state of coupled permanence *is* achievable, and as freighted with psychological interiority as we all now are, uncoupling can only be experienced as ego-crushing crisis and inadequacy. Even though such uncoupling is increasingly the norm, not the exception, the grief of failed love is exacerbated by inevitable feeling of personal failure, because the expectation is that it should be otherwise—even though technically everyone knows that as the demands put on the couple form escalated, so did divorce rates, and even knows that given the current divorce rate, all indications are that whomever you love today—the center of your universe, your little Poopsie—has a good chance of becoming your worst nightmare at least 50 percent of the time. (Of course, that's only the percentage who actually *leave* unhappy unions, and not an accurate indication of the happiness level or nightmare potential of the other 50 percent who don't.) Marriage historian Lawrence Stone suggests—rather jocularly, you can't help thinking—that today's rising divorce rates are just a modern technique for achieving what was once achieved far more efficiently by early mortality.

Nevertheless, our age dedicates itself to allying the turbulence of romance and the rationality of the long-term couple, hoping to be convinced despite all evidence to the contrary that love and sex are obtainable from one person over the course of decades, and that desire will manage to

sustain itself over thirty or forty or fifty years of cohabitation. (Should desire unaccountably sputter out, just give up
sex; lack of libido for your mate is never an adequate
rationale for "looking elsewhere.") Of course both parties
must also *work* at keeping passion alive (what joy), given
the presumption that even after living in close proximity to
someone for an historically unprecedented length of time,
you will still muster the requisite fizz to achieve sexual congress on a regular basis. (*New Yorker* cartoon husband to
cartoon wife: "Now that the kids are grown and gone, I
thought it might be a good time for us to have sex.") And
true enough, some couples do manage to perform enough
psychical retooling to reshape the anarchy of desire to the
confines of the marriage bed, plugging away at the task year
after year like diligent assembly line workers (once a week,
same time, same position), aided by the occasional fantasy
or two to get the old motor to turn over, or keep running, or
complete the trip. The erotic life of a nation of workaholics:
if sex seems like work, clearly you're not working hard
enough at it.

This modern belief that love lasts shapes us into particularly fretful psychological beings, perpetually in search of
prescriptions, interventions, aids. Passion must *not* be allowed
to die! Frequent professional consultation and attempted
cures are thus routine, seized on with desperation regardless
of cost or consequence. At least this has an economic upside:
whole new sectors of the economy have been spawned, an
array of ancillary industries and markets fostered, and massive social investments in new technologies undertaken, from
Viagra to couples porn: late-capitalism's Lourdes for dying
marriages. Like dedicated doctors keeping corpses breathing

with shiny heart-lung machines and artificial organs, couples too, armed with their newfangled technologies, can now beat back passion's death. Of course the penchant for keeping things alive through technology does have a ghoulish underside: witness the nursing homes crammed to capacity with our rotting and abandoned corpse-like elders, who spend their days aimlessly shuffling the hallways—those who can still walk, that is—muttering, "Enough already." We've all seen more than a few couples in the same condition, hooked to their weekly therapy sessions like a joint respirator, and have probably wondered how long it can be before the coroner arrives to pronounce the body dead, or whether a dignified and humane ending (someone grab a pillow) wouldn't be preferable. (*New Yorker* cartoon: husband and wife at marriage counseling. Husband to therapist: "No heroic measures.") Is beating death really worth any sacrifice? "Yes!" say the technocrats in their starchy lab coats: if every other aspect of nature can be tamed and transformed by technology, why not desire too? Desire may not have lasted a lifetime back in the old days ("The one obstacle love can't overcome is time," Denis de Rougemont says acerbically in *Love in the Western World*), but that was then and this is now: a brave new world of love.

Then there are the assorted low-tech solutions to desire's dilemmas: take advice. In fact, take more and more advice, until it's seeping out of your ears and pores. Relationship advice is a booming business these days: between print, airwaves, and the therapy industry, if there were any way to quantify the GNP in romantic counsel circulating throughout the culture at any one moment, it would certainly amount to a staggering number. There are now some 50,000 couples therapists in the nation (in addition to all the ordinary therapists who just give relationship advice on the side). Obviously maintaining a relationship nowadays is something no one should attempt to do on their own—it's far too complicated for ordinary non-trained humans, like deciding to build your own telecommunications satellite and launching it into space.

Eager to be cured of love's temporality, a desperate populace has molded itself into an advanced race of advice receptacles, like some new form of miracle sponge that can instantly absorb many times its own body weight in wetness. Check out the relationship self-help aisle in your local bookstore chain, its floor-to-ceiling advice, each book with its own complicated internal logic or complex system generally involving multipart questionnaires, acronyms, charts, and bullet points. Complete the exercise titled Your Emotional Command System Score. You will soon discover whether you are a Nest Builder, a Commander in Chief, a Sentry, or an Energy Czar. If your partner has an incompatible Emotional Command System, this explains the problems you're having. What a relief! Not only that but according to this relationship expert "such differences are based on brain circuitry, which helps you see your differences in a more objective light." The literature of bad relationships bustles with bad science and bad analogies: could there be a connection? You have your economist analogies: "Is your relationship overflowing with deposits or headed toward bankruptcy?" Your mechanical expert analogies: "You would not attempt to fix a car engine without fully understanding its complex mechanism!" And of course, your plant-foreman analogies. Consider carefully the opening line of *Fighting for Your Marriage: Positive Steps for Preventing Divorce and Preserving a Lasting Love:* "Good marriages take work." Or here's a variation on the theme from *The Relationship Cure,* which tries sneaking in the work injunctions while you're distracted: "Things to do together: Hug. Kiss. Hold hands. Wrestle. Cuddle. Have a snowball fight. Fold laundry. Clean house. . . ." (Though even the author is not persuaded by his own advice. Read on a few pages and you will come to the proviso: "And what if you don't see an immediate improvement in your relationship after following these steps? That's not unusual. . . .")

And what sort of shriveled social creature emerges from this prolonged warm bath of advice? If once brimstone and hellfire kept populations in line, now there's sudsy self-improvement. If the most devastating fear afflicting the modern individual is of losing love—or worse, not getting it in the first place—at least you can always "work on yourself" to forestall that particular dread. If failing at love puts every iota of self-worth into question, there's really only one solution. *Become more lovable.* Of course becoming lovable is your option; no one is forced to participate. But just as earlier strivers and pilgrims sought grace and afterlife salvation through obedience to an overarching power, so we subjugate ourselves to our own equally overarching power, hoping for similar payoffs, but here on earth. Your reward will come any day now: the salvation of a better relationship.

But what exactly is it about the actual lived experience of

companionate coupledom that brings on its own dissolution, that arouses the flight instinct in those very same entities once so eager to settle in for the duration, pledging themselves so optimistically to lifetime partnership and its domestic conditions? What changed? Or . . . were the seeds of dissolution there even from the start, and you somehow overlooked them? Could there have been something amiss, even in those early heady days when it was all so blissful and full of potential? Something in those mutual misrecognitions we call "falling in love," in the very excitement of connecting, something in the thrill of vulnerability and soul-bearing nakedness, something in the attraction and the *great sex* . . .

To seriously entertain questions such as these will require journeying back in time to the very beginning, to those very first stirrings of love, back to that enchanted evening when you were eating oysters and sipping champagne by candlelight (or fill in the romantic scenario and comestibles of your choice) as open and glistening as a quivering oyster on the half shell yourself, thrilling to the long tines of your lover's delicate fork piercing you in your very being, and tasting you in all your briny fullness—back to when you said those words and felt those sensations and you knew just what love meant. Note, however, that our purpose in journeying back is not sentimental, but to examine the *fundamental premises* of that moment, to take a cross section and examine it under a powerful high-intensity microscope that detects pathogens not visible to the naked eye. Be apprised that we will not at this time be taking cross sections of anyone's partner or exes or analyzing individual neuroses and shortcomings, as satisfying as this so often proves. (Satisfying not least because it's what makes serial monogamy possible: it went wrong last time because you had the *wrong person,* next time around undoubtedly it will be the right one.) Nevertheless, as for the ex's flaws or narcissism or emotional game-playing, as for what you learned about yourself and the mistakes you swear you'll never make again . . . here you're on your own.

The first slide please.

Fundamentally, to achieve love and qualify for entry into that realm of salvation and transcendence known as the couple, you must *be* a lovable person. What precisely does this entail? Let's begin with the basics. Being lovable will, of course, require an acceptable level of social normalcy: personal hygiene, a suitable wardrobe, class-appropriate social skills. Any overly evident social abnormality will likely impede your progress toward acquiring love. Conceal where possible. But normalcy just gets you in the door. According to the tenets of modern love, lovability will also require a thorough knowledge of the intricacies of *mutuality.* Neophytes beware: mutuality can prove more difficult than it looks, and occasionally hazardous. Proceed at your own pace. Don't get frustrated. Try not to compare yourself to those more experienced. That's how beginners get hurt.

Mutuality means recognizing that your partner has *needs,* and being prepared to meet them. The modern self is constituted as a bundle of needs waiting to be met, meaning that intimacy will be, by definition, rather a fraught and anxious scene. This is largely because modern intimacy presumes that the majority of those needs can and should be met by one person alone: if you question this, you question the very foundations of the institution, thus don't. Meeting someone's needs is the most effective way to become the object of her or his desire, which is what we all most yearn to be, and feel ourselves to be worthless failures if we are not.

These needs of ours do run deep however: a tangled underground morass of ancient gnarled roots looking to ensnarl any hapless soul who might accidentally trod upon their outer radices. We're born needy, these needs will never be entirely met, yet we love nothing more than our needs. Question anyone's needs and you risk losing a limb. Needs do often seem inexplicably connected to anger, generally directed at anyone who evokes them without fully meeting them, which is by definition, any intimate, since completely met needs will never be completely possible. (Needs are as much part of the past as the present.) We love our needs because they make us the individuals we are, and the individual is much vaunted in our times. We hate our needs because they're what make us oversized squalling dependent infants, and maturity—as we constantly hear—is also much vaunted in our times. Thus on a moment-by-moment basis the realm of modern intimacy often resembles nothing more than a vast nursery of hungry babies with no motor coordination or focus, each with picky preferences and different feeding schedules, each designated to provide the others with vital nourishment of the right sort and amount at the right time—and unconditionally—all the while waiting ravenously to be fed themselves.

Nevertheless, meeting another's needs is what is known as *intimacy,* itself required to achieve the state known as *psychological maturity*—despite how closely it seems to reproduce the affective conditions of our childhoods. (Trading compliance for love is the earliest social lesson learned: we learn it in our cribs.) You, in return, will have your own needs met by your partner, in matters large and small. In practice, many of these matters turn out to be quite small, indeed gnatlike, yet frequently it is these gnatlike tensions and disagreements over the minutiae of daily living that stand between couples and their requisite intimacy. Taking out the garbage, "tone of voice," a forgotten errand—these are the dangerous shoals upon which intimacy so often founders.

Thus mutuality requires *communication,* since in order to be met, these needs must be expressed. No one's a mind reader, which is not to say that many of us don't expect this quality in a mate: who wants to keep having to tell someone what you need all the time? What you *need* is for your mate to understand you: your desires, your contradictions, how past experiences have shaped who you are, your unique sensitivities, what irks you. (In practice, this means what it is about the mate that irks you.) You, in turn, must learn to understand the mate's needs: this will require being willing to *hear* what about yourself irks the mate. Hearing is not a simple physiological act performed with the ears, as you will quickly learn. You may think you know how to hear, but don't think that means you know how to *listen.* (*New Yorker* cartoon wife to cartoon husband: "Can you spare a few seconds to minimize my problems?")

Failure to listen ranks high in the compendious catalogue of couple complaints. The evidence that you know how to listen? In truth, the only valid evidence is that you undertake, upon first hearing, to immediately change, reverse, or eliminate whatever irksome trait or action is under review. Failure to do so will constitute evidence that you have not truly heard, or may even be incapable of hearing—a modern auricular disorder that will require immediate professional intervention. Experts have devised complicated but helpful therapeutic regimes to remedy such disabilities, involving curative exercises such as repeating back to the partner the exact words she or he has just spoken. Reputedly this will teach you to listen. Of course, being required to impersonate another person in order to achieve intimacy also somewhat contradicts the fundamental modern injunction to "be yourself." Can you really feel authentic as you're training your responses to conform to a mate's—often capricious and frequently unreasonable—needs? This is a perplexing question, and not the last such paradox we will encounter in our explorations: paradoxes are scattered across our path like land mines.

The protocols of companionate coupledom do typically require two individuals to coexist in an enclosed space for extended periods of time: in other words, *domesticity.* Domesticity will clearly require substantial quantities of compromise, flexibility, and adaptation simply to avoid mayhem. (Which as we have seen in cases of intimate violence, proves not always sufficiently avoidable.) Successful cohabitation requires reducing the differences between two individuals to, at the very minimum, the point of joint toleration, though often this point will not arrive until the will of at least one of the parties has been shrunken to manageable proportions, not unlike a tumor subjected to massive doses of radiation. Given the hold that post-Romantic ideals of unconstrained individuality exert over our fundamental ideologies of the self, this can prove a perilous and threatening process. Nevertheless, both parties must be willing to jettison whatever aspects of individuality might prove irritating, while being allowed to retain enough of it to feel their autonomy is not being sacrificed, even as it's being surgically excised. (Losing one's individuality is another frequently heard couple complaint, and oft-cited grounds for couple dissolution, though so is unwillingness to reshape oneself to meet the mate's needs.) The freedom to develop one's own personality in one's own way is widely regarded as a fundamental human right of the modern individual, but isn't it also what makes certain mates so incredibly difficult to get along with?

Having mastered mutuality, you may now proceed to *advanced intimacy*. Advanced intimacy will involve inviting your partner "into" your most interior self. Another fundamental premise of the modern self is the widespread if somewhat metaphysical belief in our own interiority. Whatever and wherever this "inside" is, it has now assumed a quasi-medical status, to the point of becoming our society's prevailing bodily doctrine—along with the attendant belief that whatever is in there is clamoring to get out. Leeches and bleeding served a similar purpose in previous models of the body. However, we moderns "express our feelings" in lieu of our fluids, because everyone knows that those who don't are more disease prone, and more subject to cancer, ulcers, or a host of other dire ailments.

With love as our culture's patent medicine, prescribed for

every ill—now even touted as a necessary precondition for that other great American obsession, longevity—and "opening up" required for relationship health, we willingly subject ourselves to any number of arcane quasi-medical procedures in its quest. Lovers fashion themselves after doctors wielding long probes to penetrate the tender regions. Try to think of yourself as just one big orifice: now stop clenching and relax. If the procedure proves uncomfortable, it just shows you're not open enough. Psychotherapy may be required before sufficient dilation can be achieved: the world's most expensive lubricant. (Note that psychotherapy is itself a major player, historically speaking, in this ethos of opening up, having invented the disease it conveniently exists to cure.)

Needless to say, all this opening up will leave you feeling somewhat vulnerable, lying there psychically spread-eagled, exposed, and shivering on the examining table of your relationship. But remember, it's for your own good—even if it subjects you to whatever pain, chafing, or random microbes the partner may happen to inflict on you, inadvertently, or—maybe you suspect—not. (In the annals of couple paranoia, a favored suspicion is that the partner, knowing exactly where your vulnerabilities are, deliberately kicks you there: one reason this opening up business doesn't always feel as pleasant as advertised.) As anyone who has spent much time in—or in earshot of—a typical couple knows, the "expression of needs" is not infrequently the Trojan horse of intimate warfare, since expressing needs means, by definition, that one's partner has thus far failed to meet them. Even when gently expressed, no amount of lubricant completely prevents chafing at this accusation. Nevertheless, modern intimacy would be nowhere without these acts of ritual self-exposure, along with all the sharing, the hearing, the changing. Like confession to the church, voluntary exposure is modern intimacy's foundational ritual; the command to practice it religiously is the backbone of the modern couple liturgy.

Needs (n.) 1. a deep, unfathomable reservoir of "unresolved issues," past injuries, and childhood deprivations, compounded daily, like credit card debt, by every failure on the part of a mate to instantly comprehend their particulars and magically rectify them. 2. an infinitely and exponentially expanding category, growing faster than kudzu, threatening to smother all other life forms in the vicinity.

Yes, what a thorny business *this* turns out to be. The fundamental equation of sustained coupledom: whether and how either party's *needs* are being met at any given moment by the other party. Invariably they're not, or not completely. But how could they be? Each and every need is its own Zeno's paradox, either because meeting one invariably reanimates another, or because each has its own half-life which has its own half-life and so on, or maybe because love itself just doesn't ever completely fill the constitutive lack it's called upon to fix, no matter how hard it tries. And so here we are, consigned to pursue an illusory completeness obviously impossible to attain, beset by unfulfillable longings, with our unfortunate mates designated as after-the-fact scapegoats for impossibilities not really of their own making. (Thanks mom and dad!) All too understandably, frustration gnaws at the edges of these domestic arrangements like termites feasting on your floorboards.

Not just frustration, but *anxiety*—which has a talent for appearing in multiple guises. It's extremely fond of the guise of irritation, for example the irritation of a mate who fails to act in sufficiently reassuring ways: overly independently, or selfishly, or without taking *your* feelings into account. How annoying! But scratch the annoyance and you find . . . anxiety. Because after all, what is more anxiogenic than a partner's *freedom,* which might mean the freedom not to love you, or to stop loving you, or to love someone else, or to become a different person than the one who once pledged to love you always and now . . . perhaps doesn't? (Infidelity may be the condensation of all such anxieties, but it's hardly the only venue for them. As we will see, venues abound.) Thus derives the fundamental bargain of sustained coupledom: either individual's autonomy or freedom of movement is of secondary importance compared to the other person's security and peace of mind. And thus, the rituals of modern domesticity: anxiety avoidance is so deeply structured into the fabric of domestic routine—knowing where the mate is at any moment, curfews, travel and movement restrictions, even occasional whereabouts confirmations when necessary—you might be led to think that anxiety appeasement was modern coupledom's sustaining imperative.

Of course being "checked up on" can also prove irritating, and if preventing a partner from causing anxiety is one of modern coupledom's prerogatives, preventing a partner from acting in ways that cause too much irritation is another, licensing those numerous minor "adjustments" that must be made to the behavioral patterns of our life partners. This is why recurring phrases like *"I told you I hate it*

when you . . ." or *"Can't you ever remember to . . ."* come
to comprise the leitmotif of domestic conversation. Unfortunately the success rate of such irritation-reduction techniques would appear to be low considering the frequency
with which trivial irritations acquire the status—or volume—of "important issues" in domestic culture. (You might
even be tempted to say moral crusades, to hear your neighbors go at it sometimes.) Who forgot to do which errand,
who does more or less around the house, who did what
with the toilet seat or the toothpaste cap: considering the
amount of psychological space such issues come to occupy,
irritation would seem to be domestic coupledom's default
setting. But given that a) an overly anxious partner can often
be a source of irritation, and b) a partner who apparently
doesn't *care* enough about you to stop being irritating can
be reasonably construed as a cause for anxiety—all too frequently anxiety control and irritation control will find themselves on a head-on domestic collision course.

This snake-biting-its-tail dimension of the whole anxiety-
irritation syndrome does help explain the stultifying *repeti-
tiveness* that often seems to afflict couple communication.
The "You always/I never" routine, along with certain other
less-than-charming couple conversational syndromes: nagging, sarcasm, the tactical use of the "silent treatment." But
let's not fail to notice those impressive lightning-quick couple role reversals: accuser one moment, accused the next;
Vlad the Impaler today, tomorrow the injured party. Pop
psychology supplies us with the term "power struggle," as
one way of accounting for such dynamics, though one that
certainly casts a rather Nietzschean pall over the domestic

scene. As if the will to power could really be a factor in love and coupledom! On the other hand, given the frequency of "jokes" about couples battling for the TV remote control—the favorite cultural trope for couple power dynamics (toilet seats and toothpaste caps being joke tropes for the inconsideration-irritation issue)—maybe Nietzsche really is the psychological authority who can help us comprehend the apparently insatiable capacity for couple bickering.

If anyone truly understood the consolations of defensiveness in all its most petty manifestations (and is anything more petty than the typical domestic argument?), or why humans might "enjoy being mistrustful and dwelling on nasty deeds and imaginary slights," it was Nietzsche. It's all too clear that the wellsprings of human anxiety are to be found anywhere and everywhere, including, as he so fruitfully pointed out, at the origins of moral trumping and resentment (though he liked to say it in French, *ressentiment*) about other people's capacities for independence. Every sufferer seeks a guilty agent (friends, children, spouses), some living thing upon which he can, on some pretext or other, inventively vent his affects in order to win relief: *"I suffer: someone must be to blame for it."* Defensiveness is just our futile way of trying to prevent further injury, plus our own self-aversion, which runs deep—though what defensiveness wins you in the end, or so Nietzsche predicts, is anesthesia.*

---

*Note that anesthesia comes in assorted bodily varieties: a 1999 report in the *Journal of the American Medical Association* reports that more that 43 percent of women and 31 percent of men regularly have no interest in sex, can't have orgasms, or have some other sexual impediment.

(To anyone tempted to reread *On the Genealogy of Morals* as a marriage manual, recall that poor Nietzsche did have rather a thwarted love life himself.)

The genealogy of domesticity too is hardly an innocent story, as Nietzsche should have said if he didn't. Behind every behavior reform, and behind every insecurity, lies a certain subterfuge about its own motives—and a startling capacity for tunnel vision. The desire to control inherently uncontrollable things (in this case, a mate) thus reducing the amount of uncertainty in the world is certainly understandable—but on the other hand, what's more anesthetizing than predictability? Or less of an aphrodisiac (predictability being one of the more popular stated reasons for "looking elsewhere"). Perhaps there's something inherently unsettling in the nature of love that produces this instinct for control? Because there we are, poised between anxiety control and the death drive—"tame domestic animals" in Nietzsche's apt phrase—taming our mates to secure their love (not an entirely resentment-free project on either side of the equation). Still, most of us don't intend to be heroes about our anxieties or to follow Nietzsche's little dictum that "You alone are to blame for yourself." Why blame yourself when there's a mate to blame?

Hence, *mate behavior modification*: not only companionate coupledom's favorite recreational pastime, not just another of the awkward emotional bargains that modern love commits us to, but the master key that unlocks its universe. (*New Yorker* cartoon wife to cartoon husband: "I'm not trying to change you—I'm trying to enhance you.")

Take a breath, stretch if necessary. We have now arrived

at the threshold of modern coupledom's deep structure. We are about to enter the hidden linguistic universe of companionate couples, which as we will shortly see, rests entirely on one generative phrase: *"Would you please stop doing that."*

Couple Linguistics 101: An Overview. As is true of all human languages, the language of coupledom is governed by a finite set of rules that determine what can be verbalized and how. Let's call this "couple grammar." Linguists tell us that the most fundamental categories of thought, such as time and space, differ from language to language—this is known as the Sapir-Whorf hypothesis. Each language has its own reality, which makes language a path to understanding the culture that produced it. And the reality of couple language? What preoccupations do we find reflected there?

Close observation reveals that this is a language comprising one recurring unit of speech: the interdiction—highly nuanced, mutually imposed, exceedingly trivial commands and strictures extending into the most minute areas of household affairs, social life, finances, speech, hygiene, allowable idiosyncrasies, and so on.

Sexual interdictions are, needless to say, standard. But it is the panoply of other interdictions that is actually far more revealing about the conditions of modern couplehood. From bathroom to bedroom, car to kitchen, no aspect of coupled life is not subject to scrutiny, negotiation, and rule formation. Even if not all couples employ all interdictions, *all* couples employ the interdiction form, and love means voluntary adherence to them. ("Interdiction" may not be the term employed by the individuals themselves: words like "compromise," "getting along," "flexibility," or "adjustment" are the favored euphemisms, which does help obscure the sheer number of regulations in effect at any given time.)

None of this should come as a revelation to anyone who's ever been in a couple. We're not speaking of hidden abuses of power; this is not a story about the stormtroopers coming in the middle of the night. This is something everyone coupled actively knows, and in principle, mutually consents to. Note that "mutually" also means "gender-neutral." Premodern common law may have established the right of the husband to control his wife, but modern gender relations rests on a system of *mutual* control, commands, and interdictions. (Though jurisdiction over particular spaces and practices may still be apportioned by gender: kitchens, garages, finances, or decorating are not always subject to mutual control.) If premodern wives were considered their husband's property—"coverture" was the term—in modern love, we spouses belong to each other.

Methodological note to future researchers: these data are easily replicated. Simply take a random poll of the next hundred or thousand couples you come across, preferably out of earshot of one another. Race, class, gender, age, or sexual orientation will cause minor but ultimately insignificant variations in response. Stick to basic questions about the conditions of liberty, mobility, freedom of association, or free speech in the couple. Your respondents will likely start out laughing at your naïveté, although the laughter will sound a little forced. *Freedom?* There may be an initial reluctance to discuss the gritty specifics, with protestations of loyalty and qualms about privacy (or retribution). Don't press too hard or the defensive language of "common sense" will be invoked: *"Everyone has problems!"* Be patient. Sooner or later the floodgates of complaint will open—liquor helps—and what comes hurtling out is a catalogue of strictures, commands, and punishments so unending that you will begin to wonder why no one has yet invoked the Geneva Convention when it comes to couple relations.

What follows is a brief sample of answers to the simple question: "What can't you do because you're in a couple?" (This information is all absolutely true; nothing was invented. Nothing needed to be.)

You can't leave the house without saying where you're going. You can't not say what time you'll return. You can't stay out past midnight, or eleven, or ten, or dinnertime, or not come right home after work. You can't go out when the other person feels like staying home. You can't go to parties alone. You can't go out just to go out, because you can't not be considerate of the other person's worries about where you are, or their natural insecurities that you're not where you should be, or about where you could be instead. You can't make plans without consulting the other person, particularly not evenings and weekends, or make decisions about leisure time usage without a consultation.

You can't be a slob. You can't do less than 50 percent around the house, even if the other person wants to do 100 to 200 percent more housecleaning than you find necessary or even reasonable. You can't leave your (pick one) books, tissues, shoes, makeup, mail, underwear, work, sewing stuff, or pornography lying around the house. You can't smoke, or you can't smoke in the house, or you can't leave cigarettes in cups. You can't amass more knickknacks than the other person finds tolerable—likewise sports paraphernalia, Fiestaware, or Daffy Duck collectibles.

You can't leave the dishes for later, wash the dishes badly, not use soap, drink straight from the container, make crumbs without wiping them up (*now*, not later), or load the dishwasher according to the method that seems most sensible to you. You can't use dishes directly out of the dishwasher without unloading the whole thing. You can't accumulate things that you think you just might use someday if the other person thinks you won't. You can't throw wet clothes in the laundry hamper even though there's no logical reason not to—after all, they're going to get wet eventually. You can't have a comfortable desk because it doesn't fit the decor. You can't not notice whether the house is neat or messy. You can't not share responsibility for domestic decisions the other person has made that you've gone along with to be nice, but don't really care about. You can't hire a housecleaner, because your mate is a socialist and can't live with the idea. (Or as this respondent put it: "He said, 'I couldn't live with it'; I did the math.")

You can't leave the bathroom door open, it's offensive. You can't leave the bathroom door closed, they need to get in. You can't enter without knocking. You can't leave the toilet seat up. You can't read on the john without commentary. You can't leave bloody things in the bathroom wastebasket. You can't leave female hygiene products out. You can't wash your dirty hands in the kitchen sink. You have to load the toilet paper "over" instead of "under." You're not allowed to pay no attention to what you'd simply rather ignore: your own nose hair, underarm hair, or toenails. You can't not make the bed. You can't not express appreciation when the other person makes the bed, even if you don't care. You can't sleep apart, you can't go to bed at different times, you can't fall asleep on the couch without getting woken up to go to bed. You can't eat in bed. You can't get out of bed right away after sex. You can't have insomnia without being grilled about what's *really* bothering you. You can't turn the air conditioner up as high as you want—think of the environment instead of yourself all the time. You can't sleep late if the other person has to get up early. Or you can't sleep late because it's a sign of moral turpitude.

You can't watch soap operas without getting made fun of. You can't watch infomercials, or the pregame show, or Martha Stewart, or shows in which men are humiliated in front of women or are made to play the buffoon. You can't watch porn. You can't leave CNN on as background. You can't pathologically withdraw into sports even if it's your only mode of anxiety release. You can't listen to Bob Dylan or other excesses of your youth. You can't go out to play pinball, it's regressive. You can't smoke pot. You can't drink during the day, even on weekends. You can't take naps when the other person is home because the mate feels leisure time should be shared. You can't work when you're supposed to be relaxing. You can't spend too much time on the computer. You can't play *Dungeons and Dragons*. And stay off those chat rooms! You can't have e-mail flirtations, even if innocent. You can't play computer solitaire because the clicking drives the other person crazy. You can't talk on the phone when they're home working. You can't be rude to people who call on the phone for the mate. You can't just hang up on telemarketers, you must be polite. You can't talk on the phone when they're in the room without them commenting on the conversation, or trying to talk to you at the same time. Your best friend can't call after ten. You can't read without them starting to talk, and you're not allowed to read when they're talking to you. You can't not pay attention to their presence.

You can't be impulsive, self-absorbed, or distracted. You can't take risks, unless they're agreed-upon risks, which somewhat limits the concept of "risk." You can't just walk out on your job or quit in a huff. You can't make unilateral career decisions, or change jobs without extensive discussion and negotiation. You can't have your own bank account. You can't make major purchases alone, or spend money on things the other person considers excesses, you can't blow money just because you're in a really bad mood, and you can't be in a bad mood without being required to explain it. You can't have secrets—about money or anything else.

You can't eat what you want: goodbye marshmallow fluff, hello tofu meatballs. You can't not eat meals. You can't not plan these meals. You can't not have dinner together. You can't not feel like eating what the other person has cooked. You can't bring Ding Dongs into the house. You can't break your diet. You can't eat garlic because they can't stand the smell. You can't eat butter if they're monitoring your cholesterol. You can't cook cauliflower even if you don't expect the other person to eat it. You can't use enough salt to give the food some flavor without it being seen as a criticism of their cooking. You can't refuse to share your entrée when dining out, or order what you want without negotiations far surpassing the Oslo accords. The question of which eating implement you use (or don't), the employment of the napkin, the placement of bones, pits, and other detritus, are all subject to commentary and critique. You can't blow your nose at the table. You can't read the newspaper at meals. You can't eat things that give you gas. You can't make jokes about gas.

You can't say the wrong thing, even in situations where there's no right thing to say. You can't use the "wrong tone of voice," and you can't deny the wrong-tone-of-voice accusation when it's made.* You can't repeat yourself; you can't be overly self-dramatic; you can't know things the other person doesn't know, or appear to parade your knowledge. You can't overly celebrate your own accomplishments, particularly if the mate is less successful. You can't ask for help and then criticize the mode of help, or reject it. You can't not produce reassurances when asked for, or more frequently, when they're not asked for yet expected. You can't begin a sentence with "You always . . ." You can't begin a sentence with "I never . . ." You can't be simplistic, even when things are simple. You're not permitted to employ the Socratic method in an argument. You can't have the wrong

---

*Another striking linguistic feature of couple languages is the distinctive use of tone. As in other spoken languages such as Chinese, changes in intonation will completely change the meaning of an utterance. Listen carefully to the inflection of sentences such as "How many times do I have to *say* it?" or "Could you *please* not do that." The meaning of the communication isn't in the content, it's in the intonation. In fact, a phrase like "What did you mean by *that*?" conveys nothing less than the story of the relationship itself, a virtual catalogue of disappointments or rejections or ruffled egos: even the most tone-deaf observer can re-create a couple's entire history based solely on the particular inflection of "*that*."

laugh: too loud, too explosive, too inappropriate, too silly. You can't say "cunt." You can't make penis size jokes, or laugh when others do. You can't say what you think about the mate's family. You also can't compare the mate to any of their family members, especially not the same-sex parent. You can't hold up your own family's preferable customs in anything as a model. You can't be less concerned with the other person's vulnerability than with expressing your own opinions. You can't express inappropriate irony about something the other person takes seriously. Or appropriate anger at something the other person takes casually. You can't call a handyman to repair something if they consider themselves to be "handy." You can't not be supportive, even when the mate does something insupportable. You can't analyze the cinematography in a movie that they were emotional about. You can't not participate in their mini-dramas about other people's incompetence, or rudeness, or existence. You can't make a joke that the other person could potentially construe as unconsciously aimed at them. You can't talk about (choose one): religion, politics, Germany, Israel, the class struggle. You can't tell Polish jokes. You can't make puns or tell dirty jokes, or relate overly lengthy anecdotes. You can't make jokes about bald spots, ear shape, fat, or any other sensitivity, even if you didn't know until that moment that it was an area of sensitivity. You can't talk about your crush on your shrink. You can't talk about past relationships. Or you can't not talk about past relationships, and can't refuse to reveal all the long-forgotten details when asked. You can't refuse to talk about what you talked about in therapy. But you can't "over analyze" either, or import psychological terminology into the relationship. You can't not "communicate your feelings." Except when those feelings are critical, which they should not be.

You can't say anything that makes the other person too aware of their own incompetence or failures, reflects them back to themselves in a way that is not flattering, or pulls the rug out from any of their self-idealizations. You can't question their self-knowledge, or their reading of a particular situation. You can't issue diagnoses, even when glaringly obvious. You can't be cynical about things the other person is sincere about, or indifferent to the things they're deeply interested in that seem trivial to you: style, haute cuisine, electoral politics, office gossip, the home team.

You can't have friends who like one of you more than the other, or friends one of you likes more than the other. You can't be rude to houseguests, or leave the house when house-guests are around. You can't criticize the mate to others. You can't talk about their depression in public. You can't ignore the mate when out. When the mate is having an argument with someone, you must not take the other person's side. You can't be too charming in public, especially to persons of the opposite sex (or same sex, where applicable). You can't spend more than X amount of time talking to such persons, with X measured in nanoseconds. You can't provoke the mate's jealousy. You can't talk to people who make the mate feel insecure or threatened. You can't socialize with your exes, even if you swear it's really over. You can't transgress the standards or degree of honesty or bluntness that the other person feels is appropriate in social situations. You can't not have the other person's degree of perfectionism when entertaining. Or you can't not have their degree of casualness. You can't not laugh at their jokes in public. You can't laugh at their politics in public or in private. You can't talk about politics with their relatives, or with your own, because you're not allowed to be rude in social situations even when you think rudeness is called for, unless they also think rudeness is called for. You can't be argumentative. When playing mixed doubles you can't argue about line calls.

You can't wear mismatched clothes, even in the interests of being perversely defiant. You're not allowed to wear cowboy hats. You're not allowed to make fun of your mate's cowboy hat, despite it being a ridiculous form of headwear. You can't wear sloppy clothes at home without hearing some sort of comment on it. You can't sleep in the T-shirt you've had since college, it's ratty. You can't wear plaid, even though it's bohemian. You can't go clothes shopping alone if the other person doesn't trust your taste. You can't underdress for an occasion. If known to be indifferent to such things, you're not allowed to leave the house without passing inspection. You can't wear something that makes you look too sexy (or too dumpy, or not age appropriate). You can't dress up more than the partner is dressed up; you can't be more casual. You can't wear jeans if they think jeans are tacky.

You can't drink more than X amount when out together, even if you know you can "handle it." You can't drink without the other person counting your drinks. You can't bum cigarettes because it embarrasses the mate, even though you explain about the unspoken fraternity between smokers. You can't not "fit in." You must not dance because you're a terrible dancer (according to the mate; you happen to disagree).

You can't leave a place before they're ready to go. You can't be late, even if you prefer being late. You can't dawdle. You can't lose track of time, especially when engaged in something that doesn't involve the mate, like your e-mail. You can't forget things and then go back in the house for them once the door is closed. You can't drive too fast, or faster than the mate defines as fast. You can't tailgate, you can't honk. You may not criticize the other person's driving, signaling, or lane-changing habits. You can't listen to talk radio in the car. You can't get angry when driving, or swear at other drivers. You can't return the rent-a-car without throwing out the garbage because the mate thinks it looks bad, even if you insist that cleaning the car is rolled into the rates.

Thus is love obtained.

Such commands may be acceded to voluntarily, they may be negotiated settlements, or they may be the subject of ongoing friction. You go along with them to make your partner happy, or maybe you pick your battles, but primarily you go along (and they with you) because that's how best to preserve the couple. The less reconciled either party is to "being part of the team," the more of a loner or renegade anyone might be, the more friction in the household. The point isn't to pronounce judgment on whether or which such demands are "reasonable"—because the content doesn't matter. What matters is the form. What matters is that the operative word is *can't,* and that virtually no aspect of everyday life is not subject to regulation and review, and that in modern love acceding to a mate's commands is what constitutes *intimacy,* and that the "better" the couple the more the inhabitants have successfully internalized the operative local interdictions. What were once commands are now second nature. But once again, it's your choice. Or would be, if any of us *could* really choose not to desire love.

Certainly domesticity offers innumerable rewards, this we all know: companionship, shared housing costs, childrearing convenience, reassuring predictability, occasional sex, insurance against the destabilizing effects of non-domestic desire, and many other benefits too varied to list. But if modern love has power over us, domesticity is its enforcement wing: the iron dust mop in the velvet glove. Historian Michel Foucault has argued that modern power made its mark on the world by inventing new types of enclosures and institutions—factories, schools, barracks, prisons, asylums—where individuals could be located, supervised, processed, known, subjected to inspection, order, and the clock. Although Foucault did not get around to the subject in his lifetime unfortunately, what current social institution is more enclosed than modern domesticity? What offers greater regulation of movement and time, or more precise surveillance of body and thought to a greater number of individuals?*

Exchanging obedience for love comes naturally—we were all once children after all, whose survival depended on the caprices of love. And thus you have the template for future intimacies: if you love me, you'll do what I want or need or demand to make me feel secure and complete and

---

*Considering that he'd already dealt with asylums, prisons, and sex, what could have been next? (There were intimations he was getting there—he did once remark that the best moment of love is riding home in the taxi afterward.)

I'll love you back. Thus we grow to demand obedience in our turn, we household dictators and petty tyrants of the private sphere, who are in our turn, dictated to. *"If you love me you won't argue about it."* But as we all know (far too well), the fear and pain of losing love is so crushing, and so basic to our natures, that just about any trade-off to prevent it can seem reasonable. And thus you have the psychological signature of the modern self: defined by love, an empty vessel without it, the threat of love's withdrawal shriveling even the most independent spirits into complacency (and, of course, *ressentiment*).

And why has modern love developed in such a way as to maximize submission and minimize freedom, with so little argument about it? No doubt a citizenry schooled in renouncing desires—and whatever quantities of imagination and independence they come partnered with—would be, in many respects, advantageous: note that the conditions of lovability are remarkably convergent with those of a cowed workforce and a docile electorate. But if the most elegant forms of social control are those that come packaged in the guise of individual needs and satisfactions, so wedded to the individual psyche that any opposing impulse registers as the anxiety of unlovability, who needs a policeman on every corner? How very convenient that we're so willing to police ourselves and those we love, and call it living happily ever after.

Perhaps a secular society needed another metaphysical entity to subjugate itself to after the death of God, and love was available for the job. But isn't it a little depressing to think we're somehow incapable of inventing forms of emotional life based on anything other than subjugation?

• • •

The ceiling is creaking but every time you say you hear noises overhead, your husband convinces you that you're losing your grip. The lights flicker, he says you're the only one who sees it. There's a certain atmosphere of accusation and blame pervading the household. He's irrationally jealous: at first it was flattering, now you wonder whether there's something seriously wrong with him. He's moody, alternating between charm and bossiness, solicitude and anger. He goes out at night and won't say where he's been. You start to wonder about his motives. Can anyone who has ever experienced domestic coupledom fail to notice that *Gaslight* condenses the underlying structure of every couple argument: one person trying to convince the other that differences of opinion can only be the result of a basic flaw in the other's perception of reality?

Or, maybe your husband has made a secret pact with Satan's agents to impregnate you with the Antichrist in order to advance his acting career. It's not like you haven't been supportive of his ambitions, put up with the annoying periods of self-absorption, plus the financial uncertainty, but really, this goes too far. And you haven't cared much for his choice in friends lately either, even before discovering that they're witches: they're old, nosy, frankly they smell bad, and they're spending way too much time at your place. Of course, many couples have different values—different religions, different politics—and manage to persevere. But sometimes these basic failures of judgment can make you wonder how you ever ended up together, and whether sticking it out is worth it—though doubtless you'll wind up convincing yourself that staying together for the sake of the kid is the only option. Okay, maybe he's the Antichrist, but he's yours. (This will not be the last time the phrase "for the sake of the children" makes an appearance in our discussion.)

Ira Levin, author of the novel *Rosemary's Baby* (the runaway bestseller of 1967), just happens to be the culprit behind that other enduring classic of marital horror, *The Stepford Wives* (recently re-released as it happens). Levin appears to take a rather mordant view of the couple form. (As did his audiences: both books were bestsellers and became hit movies.) In Stepford, whipping your spouse into line with your needs is the goal of married life; if you have to kill them in the process, well, we all know how irritating an overly willful spouse can be. In Stepford, husbands don't kill their wives for money or greener pastures—they like their pastures just fine, and they even want to hold onto the same wives. They'd just prefer more compliant versions and so contrive to replace them with robotic look-alikes, who enjoy sex and housecleaning far more and complain far less than the flesh-and-blood variety. Who can blame them? But lest anyone try to write off *Stepford Wives* as a protofeminist parable about gender relations and domineering husbands, watch the TV movie sequel, *The Stepford Husbands,* which relates the same story with the genders reversed. It's not only husbands who prefer compliant mates and who resort to whatever technologies are available to get them. This could be anyone's fantasy.*

Stepford Husbands—not written by Levin—does hedge more than the far darker original. While all the other wives eagerly Stepfordize their husbands and are rewarded with mates who uncomplainingly accompany

Contemporary coupledom does have its hidden risks, or so our popular culture keeps warning us. There you are, oblivious in your snug domestic cocoon until one day something "just doesn't seem right" and your whole existence unravels out from under you. Something's being threatened: your individuality, your sanity, your life. You pick up the phone and overhear a plot to violently dispatch you *(Sorry, Wrong Number)*, your husband disappears and frames you for his murder *(Double Jeopardy)*, or stages his own death then stalks you *(Deceived)*, or you stage your own death to get rid of him and he still stalks you *(Sleeping with the Enemy)*, or his dead girlfriend warns you from beyond the grave that he's trying to kill you *(What Lies Beneath)* which indeed he is: there are countless variations on coupled gruesomeness. Once in a while a movie wife does arrange to kill a husband or two, and if the genre is film noir, manages to carry through with it—*Double Indemnity, The Postman Always Rings Twice, Body Heat*—but film noir's murdered husbands are never the characters you identify with. By contrast, when wives are threatened with murder the story is always told from the wife's point of view. We in the audience—male or female—*are* the wives, we're put in the shoes

---

them on day-long furniture-buying expeditions, our heroine guiltily rescues hers at the last moment and ends up with a dolt who insists on practicing his rebound shot against the freshly painted dining-room wall—and this is treated as a happy ending. Thus we get a last minute genre shift from marital horror to marital therapeutics: "Don't try to change your mate!" "Love him for who he is!" (Filmic depictions of married life necessarily tend toward formal incoherence and abrupt genre shifts: when unable to contain their contradictions within the plot, the problem often erupts hysterically at the level of form.)

of the character-at-risk, regarding marriage through their eyes. Could we too be "Living with a Stranger"?

Oddly, there's no critical commentary about the rather obvious fact that popular culture teems with plots in which love kills, and that we're surrounded not only by the expected love stories, but equally by *anti-love* stories: for every film that ends with a happy pair in love-affirming embrace before fading gracefully to black, another shows us the anxiety, perversity, boredom, sadism, and frustration that riddle coupled life. Perhaps it's that these themes tend to genre hop—from the gothic to the supernatural to suspense to comedy—that prevents us from recognizing the anti-love film as a genre in its own right, but still, it's as if no one had put it together that there are a lot of movies featuring guys in cowboy hats and wide open spaces. It takes a certain studied ignorance to overlook such blatant cultural repetition. Is this the genre that dare not speak its name?

The existence of repeated stories and themes is never random, any more than any culture's myths and legends are accidental or spring from nowhere, which is why anthropologists get grants to go to exotic places and chronicle their cultural narratives. And why we too must regard the repetitions and figures that weave through our own cultural genres as repositories for our own latent social anxieties or structuring contradictions too, whether or not these are immediately visible to the natives. And so, in the interests of greater cultural self-understanding, we will now foray into the uncharted hinterlands of the anti-love genre, to see what we can reveal. Don't forget your compasses and flashlights: it's going to be a dark, dank journey through the swamps of the cultural unconscious, and we don't want anyone to get lost or fall over the edge.

If the love story insists that love is the pinnacle of human achievement, the path to future happiness and fulfillment—fading quickly to black once our lovers, having overcome some temporary series of obstacles, are finally united—the anti-love story is not quite so optimistic. In the anti-love film, love is fundamentally misrecognition: what looks like love or a beloved is unmasked as something or someone else entirely: usually criminal, often a murderer. (Which invariably means a narcissist and an emotional baby to boot—mate character traits with which most of us are unfortunately familiar, even when the mate in question does, technically, refrain from attempted murder.) Love is both intoxicating and delusional, but in the end, toxic: an extended exercise in self-deception. It may not have started out that way, though usually it did; the protagonist was just blithely unaware of it, a naïveté to which any of us might fall prey and probably have. But still, how could you not see what was happening under your own roof?*

---

*We should not confuse the anti-love film with the *tragic love* film: plots in which true love is thwarted because of death, duty, or some other bad turn of events. The premise of tragic love is that love should have survived, and we feel badly that it didn't *(The English Patient, Brief Encounter, Love Story, Message in a Bottle)*. The more difficult classification task are films depicting romantic failure or couple dissolution which raise doubts in order to quell them *(Kramer vs Kramer, An Unmarried Woman)*. They purport to remain confident about love as an enterprise—if you can find a better object the next time around. (Perhaps a better name for these would be "serial love" films.)

How to wrap up the narrative without leaving an audience depressed and suicidal: here is the genre's dilemma. The typical solution is the last-moment rescue of the betrayed party from the clutches of a bad love-object by a potential new love-object or helper character (as in *Gaslight*). Additionally this permits the anti-love theme to be redeemed by the more reassuring explanatory framework of wrong object-choice. The problem wasn't love itself, the problem was—once again—one bad apple. Husband married to another woman, or plotting your murder, or to abscond with your fortune? Just wash that loser right out of your hair, pick yourself up, and start over. Of course, outcomes are invariably a dilemma for any depiction of romance—traditional love films most of all. Occasionally what starts out as a love film thus mutates into an anti-love film just by violating the usual conventions of closure, thereby accidentally—or deliberately—highlighting the essential flimsiness of the whole premise. Recall the famous closing shot in *The Graduate:* once our hero abducts his true love from her wedding ceremony and ferries her onto a city bus, rather than fading to black as convention dictates, the camera holds on the seated couple for an interminable amount of screen time, leaving us to wonder—as, it seems, are they—"What the hell now?"

This is the prohibited question of the love film. *It must not be posed,* which is precisely why the strategically timed fade-to-black is the love film's signature shot. If such questions became routine, how could affective life as we know it even proceed? If the camera kept rolling, who knows what horrors we'd see? Thus the most determined anti-love films begin where the fade-to-black leaves off. Ida Lupino's *The*

Bigamist (Lupino directed, and played one of the betrayed wives); Bergman's *Scenes From a Marriage;* Mike Nichols's *Who's Afraid of Virginia Woolf* (from the Pinter play): all grisly domestic horror shows in sharp focus. Polanski's *Bitter Moon* deserves special mention here for such an unblinking and perverse look at love unraveling into hatred that even hardened cynics will flinch and turn away.

Television (at least in its pre-cable incarnation) has traditionally tended to veil such themes, usually behind humor. In contrast to movie husbands, who seem to want to maim or kill their wives a disproportionate amount of the time, TV husbands are typically inept bumblers fearful of their over-controlling wives. Who wouldn't cower before these self-certain hausfraus: so incessantly pedagogical, spending the majority of any episode mocking hubby's incompetence, putting him in his place, moralizing, and threatening to cut off sex if he doesn't shape up. It goes without saying that women are the sexual gatekeepers, except in sitcom parodies like *Married . . . With Children*, which get a lot of comic mileage out of the premise that a woman would actually want to have sex with her husband.

Which brings us, finally, to the marriage joke, the domestic sitcom's progenitor and an example of the anti-love genre par excellence. Would stand-up comedy even exist without the figure of the spouse to aim jokes at? Consider the content of a typical marriage joke:

Two cannibals sit beside a large fire, after eating the best meal they've had in ages. "Your wife sure makes a good roast," says the first cannibal. "Yeah," says the second. "I'm really going to miss her."

The perfect combination of wishing and aggression, condensed into a toothy parody of the family meal.

Jokes are the royal road to a cultural unconscious, according to Freud, in the most interesting and unfunny book ever written on humor. Here is Freud's favorite marriage joke:

A wife is like an umbrella—sooner or later one takes a cab.

Explanation: men marry to protect themselves from the temptation to visit prostitutes, just as an umbrella is supposed to protect against rain. But the sexual satisfactions of marriage, like an umbrella in a thunderstorm, just aren't protective enough. In a downpour, sooner or later you're going to find yourself in a public vehicle.

Freud had a few other pointed things to say on the subject, for example: "One does not venture to declare aloud and openly that marriage is not an arrangement calculated to satisfy a man's sexuality, unless one is driven to do so perhaps by the love of truth and eagerness for reform." Hence the need for jokes (indirect routes to honesty), because it's impossible to completely stifle the little voice within us that "rebels against the demands of morality." Advancements in the sphere of gender equity mean that women too can now openly suffer—and joke about—sexual frustration, penis size jokes being a favored idiom. Or there are feminist jokes like "A woman needs a husband like a fish needs a bicycle," which rely on the same joke techniques—ellipsis, absurdity—as Freud's umbrella joke.

Kill them with laughs or for the insurance: either way, spousal antagonism finds the requisite cultural outlets. Given the various genres devoted to venting household aggression, given these howls of protest lodged deep within our most mainstream cultural forms, given our apparent fascination with all the violent ways that intimates can be dispatched—both fictional and actual, in the headlines or in the movies—ours would seem to be a culture more at odds with its own dictates about love than it cares to openly acknowledge.

Clearly the downside of modern love's regimes is that lingering odor of the police station, which can be hard to get out of your hair and clothes. It's something we incessantly "joke" about; it's why the phrase "ball and chain" is a synonym for spouse; it's why the fundamental premise of the marriage joke is that couples are a prison, spouses each other's jailers, and house arrest the basic condition of modern love. (*New Yorker* cartoon: man watches TV as wife makes dinner. Caption: "Life without Parole.") Social theory isn't only the province of sociologists and pointy-headed intellectuals (or adulterers either, though there may be overlaps), it's also the province of comedians, because jokes are the favored delivery system for political ideas and social critique on censored subjects. These succeed as jokes, says Freud, through their technique, but more importantly, when they articulate banished or socially risky thoughts, while also allowing us to "laugh it off"—to have the pleasure of acknowledging something and disavowing it at the same time. Jokes that don't tell some sort of truth don't get laughs. Censored truths always get the biggest laughs. (Just coming out and saying it gets no laughs at all, you only get withering looks. What's your *problem?*)

Comedian: I've been wondering: who has more freedom, a bachelor in China or a married guy in the U.S.? I have to say the bachelor in China. He may not have a passport, but at least he can go out when he wants. Me, I can leave the country, I just can't leave my house.

Apparently, banished thoughts include comparing the unfreedoms we subscribe to in personal life and the unfreedoms we oppose in political life. Or as another noted comedian, Isaiah Berlin, once put it: If an individual votes himself into slavery and thus gives up his freedom, is this really political liberty?

Peals of laughter (and disavowal?) from the land of housebound passport holders.

Chapter Three

THE ART OF LOVE

adulterate (v). 1) To debase by adding inferior materials or elements; make impure by admixture; use cheaper, inferior, or less desirable goods in the production or marketing of (any professedly genuine article).
—Random House Unabridged Dictionary
of the English Language

So are you the type who hadn't realized how unhappy you'd been until you found yourself in the midst of a serious life-shattering affair, diving headlong into this new person's arms to escape the rising tide of emotional deadness at home and in some ridiculously short space of time risking things you never thought you'd risk, without a clue how you've gotten yourself into this whole thing or what disasters might be waiting around the next corner (or the next credit card bill)? If not, please use your imagination: imagine that every moronic love song is drilling a pathway directly to your deepest self, imagine being hurtled up and down the entire gamut of emotions from one hour to the next, consuming Tums like Raisinets, but what if it's a million times more compelling than anything else in your life? Even if home life wasn't *totally* terrible, even if there were (and are) good times plus all the comforts of familiarity and history and even affection—when not squeezed out by a festering accretion of disappointments and injuries or that low-hanging cloud of overfamiliarity which means knowing in advance the shape of every argument before it even happens, and everything you once liked best about yourself getting buried under the avalanche of routine. Let's say there's even sex—reliably satisfying, gets-the-job-done sex (and what's wrong with that?)—but how can that compare to the feeling of being *reinvented?* Of being *desired?* Of feeling *fascinating?*

Or maybe you're the type who dived headlong into this love affair—possibly not for the first time?—as a rickety lifeboat from an entirely familiar unhappiness that you can't bring yourself to do anything about, and whose bittersweet romance with your own melancholia or extended penance for imagined sins (early religious training never stops rearing its head for some) will be your new lover's real competition, not that mate waiting at home. But even having made your bed you'd still prefer a little company in it now and then, plus the occasional rush of possibility all the while knowing that eventually the sackcloth will come out and there you'll be, as penitent as the day is long, slinking back to the familiar emotional deep freeze that you can't (or won't) forsake.

Or maybe you weren't unhappy at all, and things were just fine at home, and you were just unlucky enough to fall in love.

Whatever your type, however it started, the point is that you didn't *plan* to feel this way, it just happened—well maybe you didn't plan not to either, or didn't have the foresight and "maturity" to put the brakes on before it was too late; and if you started spilling the most intimate details about your relationship problems after a couple of drinks, and lately seem to be fantasizing out loud about the future in ways that are clearly rash, and venturing onto emotional limbs that might crack under your combined weight, and saying things you probably shouldn't because they do have rather a promissory air *("I've been waiting my whole life to meet someone like you" "I've never felt this way about anyone before"),* or an increasing number of those marathon confessional lovers' tell-alls contain rueful yearning sentences beginning with the phrase "If you and I lived together . . ." or references to foreign locales to which idyllic future visits might be arranged; if there's been more than one discussion of respective tastes in furniture or décor and potential agreements or arguments over (even style dissensions can have something charming about them when tinged with eros, something your mate has yet to comprehend) along with fantasized—perhaps enacted?—introductions to best friends or nonjudgmental family members (*"You'd really love my sister"*), or extended discussions of your plight with said friends and family members; it's just because you haven't felt *connected* to anyone for so long. And because you can't believe your luck in nabbing such an amusing, sexy, and adoring lover, and for the moment the bliss is edging out the anxiety about where all this is going to lead—although maybe you've had an occasional stomach-churning moment too, and a full night's sleep is a distant memory.

"Bliss": often synonymous with intense sexual reawakening—or for a few of us late bloomers, an erotic initiation (who knew it could feel this way!)—that has you stumbling around in states of altered consciousness and electrified embodiment; that has you fantasizing about sex: a) when you wake up in the morning, b) shower, c) drive to work, d) work, e) confer with the boss, f) take meetings, g) make household arrangements with the partner, h) dine *en famille* or with friends, i) try to get work done after dinner because you got none done during the day because you were lost in sex reveries. All of which means that the entire concept of "life as usual" has taken on a radical new dimension; it's a whole new sexy way of existing in the world. Granted, "newness" doesn't mean that there isn't a certain conventionality about it also. But conventional is not how it feels when you're in the midst of it.

It feels *fun*. It feels *rebellious*. Instead of Bartleby hunched dutifully over that project or report that was due days or weeks ago, there you are on the computer composing witty novella-length e-mails to your beloved. Every time you hit "send" you're redirecting resources: your productivity, your attention, the boss's dollar. Rebellion? It's virtually industrial sabotage. From upstanding citizen to petty thief: pilfering from the company stockroom, poaching in the boss's pond, as useless to the forces of production as a lovestruck hormonal teenager or a Romantic poet—no, you're hardly going to make Employee of the Year this way. You're in a state of perpetual exhaustion, raw and unmoored, up half the night either tossing and turning, or huddled in a closet or guest bathroom whispering away on the phone; days are spent in a pleasant sleepy fog, alert enough only to plot your next assignation. Or you're gabbing on the phone all day, meaning late, late nights finishing what you never got done at work and which is—oh shit!—due tomorrow. But who cares? What a blast it is feeling so unfamiliar to your-self: a tightrope walker, an explorer, a neo-virgin, a Words-worth. You're a dust-bowl farmer whose dry scrubby fields have been transformed into lush verdant plains by a miracle rainfall, vitality coursing through your thirsty back rows where only shortly ago barrenness and despair prevailed. You're remaking the world through emotions and desire, which is a full-time job in itself. *Fuck work.*

"Fuck work": if adulterers ever adopt a slogan, this could be it. A close contender: *"stolen moments."* Yes, what a dumb cliché. But consider what the slogans and clichés reveal about the nature of the experience. You don't have to be some sort of Heidegger to discern that being is indeed closely linked to time, and adultery does nothing if not dis-combobulate your temporality.* To wit: was ever a wrist-watch more assiduously ignored than when in the midst of an illicit affair? Caught in adultery's throes, even the most punctilious clock-punchers begin running perpetually late, missing appointments, double-booking, showing up half-way through dinner parties—even leaving watches behind in places they had no business being to begin with. (Rushed exits: tough on accessory-retention rates.) Basically, you'll risk just about anything for an extra half hour with the new beloved, which somehow becomes forty-five minutes, or an hour, or you've dozed off and—*"Oh my God, what time is it?"* Which means you've become a specialist of everyday

---

*Martin Heidegger: big twentieth-century philosopher and another notorious adulterer. (Main squeeze: philosopher Hannah Arendt.)

ruses once home, coughing up complex and instantaneous explanations for those mysterious gaps in the day's chronology, those stolen troves of *temps perdu*. For accuracy's sake, let us note that these are moments not precisely stolen, however, but available "for a price," this being (as all with experience in the illicit dalliance trade know all too well) *deception.* Or "excuses" or "explanations"—choose whatever term rankles least, because you'll be forking them over at exorbitant rates just to buy back your own "free time," which will be parceled back to you in paltry insufficient increments. (Note the irony.)

From upstanding citizen to crafty embezzler: siphoning off ever-larger increments of this precious commodity, *time,* from its rightful owners—mate, job, children, housepets—to cash out elsewhere like stashes of hard currency in a faltering economy, like a gambler scraping to come up with the next bet to stay in the game, because *something* in these filched moments has become vital to sustain you through all the other moribund moments that comprise your daily existence. The more infatuated you are, the more you're willing to pay; for a mere "free" evening, risking exposure, reputation, property, and . . . well, let's not think about it. The more seamless the deception, the more convincingly delivered, the more sizable the temporal increment purchased in return. You'll be needing to work late a lot *("Don't wait up!")*; suddenly the car needs numerous repairs; errands seem to multiply; an out-of-town trip is furtively extended for a day. Or you've taken up an exercise regime meaning regular trips to the gym, or are researching something that requires extensive visits to the library (your family tree? a cure for Alzheimer's?), or—surely there must be other places you have to be where cell phones are typically not in use. What about church?

"Free time." What a lie! (Though it may be uncompensated.) No, time is a finite resource, as you'll soon discover now that your greatest desire is to transfer vast sums of it into the account of a new love. Hey, you adulterers: running late? Historical footnote: flouting the rhythms of industrialism has long been a recurrent form of resistance, at least since modernity introduced time-management and government by clocks. Say hello to your predecessors: hoboes, bohemians, beatniks, hippies, and slackers. You're in illustrious company here: note too that it was the Romantics—Wordsworth and friends—who first mounted protests against the burgeoning domination of the world by timekeeping and industry—presciently too, even before their insinuation into every corner of non-work life, from leisure to love. Recall Wordsworth's *Prelude,* a polemic against—

> *The Guides, the Wardens of our faculties,*
> *   and Stewards of our labour, watchful men*
> *And skilful in the usury of time,*
> *Sages, who in their prescience would controul*
> *All accidents, and to the very road*
> *Which they have fashion'd would define us down,*
> *Like engines . . .*

Regulating temporality was the necessary precondition for reconciling humans, with our messy individualities and errant desires, to the demands of industry, and crucial in establishing the modern factory system itself: adherence to clock time was—and is—the bottom-line requirement for producing a pliant workforce. Historian E. P. Thompson points out that the spread of clocks was itself symptomatic of a new Puritan discipline and a corresponding bourgeois exactitude, but it was industry that imposed strictures like fines, bells, whistles, and time clocks, foisting a new inner consciousness of time on a hitherto untimely population. (And with the outer strictures came a new moral rhetoric around punctuality, preaching the virtues of Work, Frugality, Order, and Regularity.) The result? We're the result: time organizes us as selves, from the inside out—not just the earliest lesson anyone learns in utilitarian thinking, but one so successfully internalized that bells and whistles are entirely unnecessary. Bourgeois exactitude is the temporality of our deepest self. Which means that even small protests against time-management are worth some attention, because screw around with time and, in fact, you're adulterating the very glue of orderly social existence.*

But if stumbling into the wrong bed with the wrong partner and getting lost in reverie and losing track of time refashions ordinary citizens into default social critics and heirs to Romantic protest, if adultery's transgressions aren't confined to the bedroom but threaten to leak into all the adjacent rooms too—first the household, and then there goes the neighborhood—then, perhaps social conservatives and marital moralizers are onto something when they fret about sexual transgression. Maybe there really is some sort

---

*Consider here the suspicion that certain minority groups have an insufficiently respectful or even rebellious attitude toward timekeeping, as expressed anxiously (or enviously) in numerous majority group jokes on the subject.

of domino effect, and the social fabric *is* being irrevocably sullied and torn asunder (just as the doomsday pamphleteers and sexual-abstinence crowd like to prophesize) which would make adultery far more than a tiny howl of protest against the tick tock inevitability of "how things are." It's one step away from compete insurrection.

Or maybe not. But whatever political valence anyone wants to assign to sexual transgression—not an uncontested question on either the right or the left—at least we can say without risking an argument that it's a thorn in the side of a conservative vision of collective social life. But what a contradictory issue transgression is generally for the culture-at-large, which certainly has a big approach-avoidance complex about it—quite the love-hate relationship. When safely segregated in museums or ghettoized in the gallery districts, transgression is much celebrated by art patrons and aesthetes for its liberating expressivity; its practitioners lauded for their rule-defying panache and daring imagination. A mustache on a Mona Lisa, a signed urinal in a museum: when stamped with the imprimatur of Art and the Romantic myth of talent, all sorts of violations—aesthetic and social—can be regarded as their own sphere of inventiveness; rebellion and bad behavior much admired as privileged domains of truth and insight. This is modernity's sanctioned method for delivering calculated aesthetic jolts to mired sensibilities. All of this is by now well established under labels like "avant garde" or "modernism," or these days, "postmodernism"; so is the practice of isolating such endeavors in the equivalent of petting zoos to which the culturati flock on weekends to admire the wildlife and cadge a few frissons.

But why should disrupting conventions be the province of artists alone? Why should poets and painters get all the fun, and shocking the bourgeoisie be left to poseurs with grants and fancy art school degrees? Why can't everyone experiment with possibilities, and invent new ways of seeing or toy with transgression and get congratulated for it? The evacuation of creativity from ordinary work and its reassignment to the artist classes may have been an unfortunate turn of history—a by-product of the social division of labor ushered in by those very same time-management mavens of industrialization—but it does *not* have to be adhered to forever. Ditto the habit of imagining that art and life are autonomous spheres and artists a separate, privileged breed. This is merely a convention of thinking, not an independent fact of existence. If we've learned anything from our various avant gardes and their assorted motley movements—that is, before they got co-opted and conservative, before they abandoned life to cower in museums— isn't it that all mainstream institutions are sitting ducks for artful saboteurs, that all social forms invite creative violations and sneak attacks from whatever factions or movements happen along to disrupt their smug dominance? Religion has its blasphemers, the military its mutineers, consumerism its shoplifters, mandatory education manufactures truants, and as we've seen, entering into domesticity creates—or invites—the conditions for adulterating it. Clearly, wellsprings of avant gardism are pulsating everywhere beneath the faux conventionality and skin-deep rule adherence of "normal life"—there's just not a market for it. No patrons, no commissions, no Castelli or Christie's. Though anyone ever forced to take a modern art history course will note that the theme of adulteration—the act, its threat, its opponents, its celebration—has motored just about everything that counts as significant in art and aesthetics for at least the last century, and will perhaps note too the structural similarity with certain other less-lauded (and less-contained) modes of adulteration such as those under consideration here.* Of course when it comes to creative expression, the official aesthetic sphere itself has long ceased to be governed by visuality alone: envisioning and re-visioning of every sort goes on here; adulterations both conceptual and psychological are well established in the expressive canon, just as the terrain of personal life itself has long been mined as subject matter and entire new genres feed off the self and its revelations.

Conversely, perhaps adultery itself is not without a certain aesthetic dimension: consider its untidy materiality, its permeable boundaries, the multiple perspectives and ocular confusions it leaves in its wake. Conventions are defied; chance elements introduced; new viewpoints engineered. Consider the spectatorial position of the third party, for instance, both participant and audience for aesthetic transgressions galore: the Marcel Duchamps of domestic life. As third party, you'll get to see all *sorts* of things (and maybe even defile a few of them too). You may happen to one day find yourself touring the family domicile, for instance, allowing opportunities to explore closets, medicine chests, or refrigerators; to view family photographs if that's your thing; to rifle mail and peruse the bookshelves. You may

---

*The key text would be Clement Greenberg's influential essay "Avant Garde and Kitsch" (1939), kitsch here playing the adulterer role.

have occasion to sleep—or whatever—in the nuptial bed. If there are children, you will become conversant with their problems, achievements, and rebellions. You may attend social functions at which the spouse is present, knowing that you know his secrets while he doesn't know yours. (Or so you presume. Recall that in Pinter's *Betrayal* the husband knew all along; the wife just forgot to mention it to her lover—coincidentally the husband's best friend—who only finds out years later.) Flouting marital rule, even with discretion, *is* always messy, invariably deranging domestic quiescence, even if invisibly. But then messiness has certain aesthetic attractions too (now you're the Jackson Pollock of domestic life), particularly as a response to the overly ordered existence, to sparkling households and "maintaining appearances," and the daily repetition of known-in-advance outcomes.

Or consider triangulation: adultery's aesthetic trademark. Like some vast earth sculpture, rearranging the most fundamental geometry of organized social life—the couple form—from dyad to triad, revamping the contours and infrastructure of modern intimacy itself. About triangulation there is far too much to be said. Modern art history factoid: when Surrealist artist Max Ernst donated a pair of his wife Marie-Berthe's discarded, white high-heeled shoes to his then-mistress, artist Merit Oppenheim (creator of that celebrated Surrealist *objet,* the fur-covered teacup, saucer, and spoon), Oppenheim refashioned the shoes into a sculpture titled *My Nurse.* Coming across her own discarded shoes on display in a Parisian Surrealist exhibit a few years later, Marie-Berthe attacked and destroyed the piece.

Aren't all we adulterers amateur collagists? We're scavengers and improvisers, constructing odd assemblages out of detritus and leftovers: a few scraps of time and some dormant emotions are stuck together to create something unforeseen, to have new experiences. We're default parodists too, even if unintentionally: the social framework invariably gets a good dose of mocking, considering all those opportunities for propriety violations. (The most effective parodists are always insiders: it takes a thorough knowledge of the logic of the system to sabotage its most cherished illusions, to artfully expose its strains and weak points.)

Let's return to that fundamental propriety violation, the *domicile visit*. Caution: these can prove unexpectedly messy. This is because people themselves can be unexpectedly messy, in all senses of the word. Those accustomed to moving through the world with physical grace develop sudden attacks of clumsiness: the bric-a-brac teeters; porcelain is in jeopardy. Normally well-organized types undergo mysterious bouts of forgetfulness: accessories are misplaced and various traces of your physical existence "somehow" left behind. Kleptomania is not an unknown occurrence even among typically non-thieving populations: why not a souvenir or two? But do beware: houses, furniture, and even appliances prove to have loyalties and memories, they sprout eyes and ears, they can and will betray your secrets like something out of a Stephen King novel. Recall the crucial role played by a vacuum cleaner in *Sex, Lies, and Videotape,* a movie whose narrative turning point comes when an earring "lost" by one sister, Cynthia, in the bedroom of the other, Ann—lost, that is, in the course of an afternoon escapade involving Cynthia and Ann's husband, John—is discovered some time later by Ann, clogging the vacuum nozzle, and Ann realizes instantly how it got there. Or take caution from the tale of B., normally a laid-back and considerate fellow, entreated to the domicile of his married paramour J. for dinner one night (the husband is conveniently out of town on business). Everything is going well until the two fall into desultory post-dinner conversation on a subject about which neither is particularly informed or even deeply interested (Western versus holistic medicine); the phrase "Oh, don't be silly" is voiced by J. in response to one of B.'s more tenuous assertions, which escalates into a fight, which culminates in B. punching his fist through the dining-room wall. He has no idea what came over him! The husband is returning the next day; a frantic search for a twenty-four-hour plasterer ensues. (A nonexistent occupational category, as it happens.)

Or consider the case of C., victim of another such household "accident." C.—who has generously offered to baby-sit for the sick child of friends whose baby-sitter has quit unexpectedly and they both have work situations that must be attended to—happens to be sleeping with one of the parents. Which one doesn't matter for our purposes. All that matters is that C. is genuinely happy to help (even relieved to help: good deeds are a fungible currency in the parallel guilt economy), though in the course of removing a pot of soup from the refrigerator to heat up for the sick child, "accidentally" upturns it. Pea soup. In the refrigerator. A pot of pea soup cascading through a refrigerator's white-on-white environs, penetrating every crevice and niche with gloppy green goo, will simply never come completely clean. The pea soup crust in that refrigerator will outlast the affair, and probably the marriage. Moral: houses and appliances are not to be trifled with.

Even when steering clear of the domicile itself with its malevolent appliances and just-asking-for-it walls, domestic life will still exert its influence over you, the third party, adulterating your existence too in any number of unexpected ways. You may find yourself involved in household business and errands; you may be introduced to the lover's friends who may or may not be in on the secret; you may discuss the situation with those friends, who will, of course, have their own vicarious investments in it (or who will be uneasily aware that you have likely been let in on their little secrets too). Your own daily life will be shaped by the absent mate's moods, job, travels, colds, yeast infections, meal schedules, and propensities to jealousy, suspicion, or cell phone calls at inopportune moments. And vice versa: it's not as if your actions don't register in the other direction. In fact, this person's well-being lies smack in your hands. Do you kindly protect an unsuspecting partner from the secret you know could shake his or her world, or do you find yourself (perhaps "unconsciously") complicit in organizing its discovery. Easy to call at the wrong moment; to fail to wake your lover in time to get home at the appointed hour; to leave telltale signs in or on body, clothing, car; to neglect to point out when the lover is acting "carelessly." (More on this interesting little syndrome to come.)

Of course it goes without saying that all adulterers are routinely exposed to the most privy aspects of each other's primary relationships. What else is post-coital conversation for? It's a keyhole vantage into coupled privacy and one accessible from this location alone—the adultery bed—

because one couple member has turned saboteur, handing over the blueprints to the vault. Secrets are spilled; embarrassing truths are revealed; privacy norms are out the window. Lovers reveal to each other what they don't dare say elsewhere, sometimes not even to themselves. Perhaps love affairs are for saying the unsayable. (At least that's the admission ticket: *"I'm lonely." "I'm bored." "Come to my room."*) Whatever the mechanics, you third parties will invariably find yourselves in possession of a small arsenal of intimate data on the particularities of the "other" relationship. Depending on your lover's volubility or discontent, or your own propensities for asking direct questions or making inferences, *everything* is soon known: an illustrated catalogue of complaints, an unabridged history of couple arguments, many years' accumulation of disappointments and betrayals, and a psychological profile on the absent mate with a level of detail rivaling one of Freud's case studies. This is a person you may never meet, but will come to know very well: every neurosis, small and large; every annoying habit, tic, rigidity, or unreasonable expectation; every less-than-charming idiosyncrasy. Though should you have occasion to meet—or perhaps you already have?—these impressions may need to be revised; obviously, you're only hearing "one side of the story." *

But nothing creates instant intimacy like the spousal

---

*You may indeed have met. Yes, straying within a couple's social circle does occasionally happen, and in the dynamics of these encounters, the absent mate is never all that absent. Let's be frank: is there something a little arousing about that too? We're born into triangulation after all; perhaps it never entirely ceases to be a compelling scenario for this reason.

complaint, and being on the receiving end of your lover's ambivalence about the figure who is, after all, your rival; vested with the inside scoop on the private inferno of coupled woes or coupled somnambulance, knowing that you alone are the respite from your lover's malaise—as you're assured in those whispered phone calls, those agonized e-mails—well, it can be quite seductive, can't it? The mate's faults become a conversational staple and every fresh anecdote and domestic injustice draws you two all that much closer. She's bitter, he's emotionally unavailable; their waistlines are expanding, their sex drives diminishing. (It goes without saying that they've lost interest in sex, or were never very interested to begin with, or won't put out, or only on schedule, or are sexually unimaginative, or barter, or won't do X—or certainly not nearly as well as you.) Coupled life is either a barren landscape or a tense battleground or a nightmarish repetition, characterized variously by tedium, fighting, silence, or unreasonable insatiable demands. All of which may even provide you, the "other person," with opportunities for gracious beneficence, to be the "better person"—reasonable, less neurotic. A helpmate. You may even occasionally find yourself arguing the mate's side, becoming a behind-the-scenes adjudicator in domestic quarrels, offering counsel, insights, therapist referrals. Why not be gracious, after all? If it's an implicit competition—though that does make it sound a trifle undignified—as long as those complaints continue, apparently you're winning it. (Of course spousal complaints may have a certain adhesive quality too, especially when chronic—the pressure release valve that keeps the system operative. But we're getting ahead of our story.)

Not all those who stray do complain about their mates.

Many are circumspect and even loyal in their fashion: liking, respecting, loving a mate while still "wanting more" is not unknown in the annals of human desiring. But if coupledom is society's sanctioned store-all for intimacy, property, children, and libido, then adultery is the municipal Dumpster for coupled life's toxic waste of strife and unhappiness. Helpful hint to you "other" guys and gals: on those occasions when you do find yourself sifting through the smelly couple trash with your lover: make sure that those tetanus shots are up-to-date. Rubbish-picking can have its hazards. You never know what you're going to come across, so watch your step. It's easy to stumble into something nasty, lose your bearings, and end up with a contact rash.

But even sans complaint, boundaries still begin to crumble, the colors start to run. Meaning that you will also become sexual intimates with this absent mate over time, or will in a manner of speaking. And here we come to the real messy materiality of triangulation. You may not have met the person, but, after all, you're sharing many things. It's not just that certain sexual details may be confessed, or vented, or inferred, but that the presence of the mate's body is registered in precise detail upon your own. You're having a sexual whirl because the mate has lost interest, is depressed or on antidepressants, too angry or too ambivalent, or impotent or frigid. But also because—let's be frank—in any long-term sexual relationship, techniques and rhythms are developed in response to the partner's body and preferences. Now enter you, Partner Number Two. Being made love to as though you inhabited someone else's sexual penchants does put you on rather sexually intimate terms, as the erotic preferences of another body are mapped out for you on your own. Or maybe those acts the mate isn't too keen for take on a certain centrality in your new erotic life. Subtly prompted—or requested—by a variation-hungry lover? Meanwhile, on the other side of the equation, you, the straying partner, make love to your new lover with the pleasure—but also, at times, the chagrin—of unfamiliarity, mapping the similarities and differences as you go. You're rediscovering your forgotten capacities—and acts, and desires—but at the same time, comparing, measuring, playing catch-up, and invariably registering the absent presence of that other very familiar body, the one that shares your bed when you finally return to the domestic fold, for sleep if nothing else. Though sometimes for something else as well? How awkward to return home from the adultery bed to find an unexpectedly amorous spouse awaiting! Though perhaps reassuring too? After all, routines become routine because they work, and yes, reliability has its pleasures, too.

Speaking of overlaps and leaks: is there an adulterer so successfully compartmentalized that images of the lover are not occasionally—perhaps frequently—summoned as a nuptial aid? Yes, employing the lover's body as a prop to reconsummate a flagging domestic sex life. This may work, though it may also abruptly stop working, and you may find yourself feigning sexual enjoyment like an aging prostitute with the last customer of the night hoping it will just be over soon. Or worse, finding yourself unable to feign and rummaging around for an appropriate excuse, or even worse than that, growing detached from the experience and secretly critical *("Must I really listen to that same little noise once again at exactly the same moment?")* with a running inner monologue that won't shut up. Or the partner's body

is beginning to seem just a little off-putting and you're starting to notice and become irked by various bathroom or
grooming or consumption routines or bodily anomalies ("*Who
on earth has hair growing* there?") or those little physical habits that were once endearing or just matters of indif-
ference are now becoming a little . . . disgusting. These are
definitely bad signs. You may read them as indicating that
"things" have become rather less manageable than you had
hoped. ("Out of hand" is the usual phrase.) Though as
Freud points out, desire and disgust *are* only a hair away
from each other—or rather, only as far away as the sex
organs from the elimination functions. Yes, in the Freudian
view, sexual disgust is the anatomical destiny we're forever
staving off in the sphere of love, and too bad for us, less and
less successfully as the romance fades—or perhaps that's
why it does.*

---

*Freud's universalizing picture of disgust contrasts with more historical
accounts such as Norbert Elias's in *The History of Manners*. Based on his
reading of early modern etiquette manuals (which suddenly began frown-
ing on previously accepted behaviors like blowing your nose into your
sleeve, or started instructing on where and when one can break wind),
Elias traces the expansion and transformation in levels of sensitivity and
delicacy around bodily functions to this period—noting too that these
newly heightened strictures and refinements will subsequently become
internalized as feelings of shame and embarrassment, soon to become the
linchpins of the modern psyche. In other words, where Freud saw disgust
in terms of individual development (children aren't disgusted by their
body products, indeed they enjoy playing with them; repression only
kicks in later), Elias transposes the development story onto Western culture. Needless to say, both accounts find their critics, but the fact that
disgust is a shadow presence in the travails of contemporary intimacy
and sexual attraction seems pretty indisputable.

And let's not forget self-disgust. It might be mentioned that deceiving intimates doesn't always prove the happiest circumstance when it comes to thinking well of oneself: those stolen moments can have their price. Though you occasionally hear it said that a certain amount of mutual deception can be tolerated if it sustains long-term coupledom, Americans tend to refer to this as the "European" attitude, that is to say, a distant and slightly unwashed concept. (In fact, a recent survey on attitudes toward monogamy in France found them to be identical to those of Americans.) But given the moral onus attached to the subject of couple deception, given the representatives of the animal kingdom or parts of the lower body its practitioners will be likened to, contemplating these questions at all may require various self-image cushioning devices: alcohol typically, often accompanied by a medley of self-justifications on auto-play trilling away back in the old reptile brain. ("Infrequent domestic sexual contact" has long since gone platinum, permanently perched at the top of the hit parade.)

But let's admit that honesty is itself a topic riddled with deception, which makes any sustained self-reflection on it tricky. The fact is that collective social life demands deception from all of us on a regular basis and no one can claim virgin status here. (Is there anyone who has never called in sick when not, strictly speaking, sick, or when the relative in question is, strictly speaking, still alive? Never begged off a social engagement with some creative alibi because the time could be otherwise utilized, even if utilized doing nothing?) Deception is hardly rare as we wend our way through the vagaries of the social world with its sticky interpersonal demands and double bind situations. Every socialized being knows that a certain amount of lying is fundamental to collective existence *("You look great"; "I'll call you")* and is probably also aware that sociality as we know it would come grinding to a halt without it. You don't have to be Oscar Wilde to know that maintaining friendships, holding down a job, dealing with relatives or in-laws, or sometimes just getting through the day frequently requires recourse to some version of false self.

Actually, collective life demands far more elaborate forms of deception from us than social lying alone: a significant degree of self-deception is also required. (The self-deception of thinking of yourself as an "honest person" while engaged in these fundamental social deceptions is optional.) Social scientists who study deception report that not only is deceiving others automatic social behavior, a willingness to *be* deceived is equally automatic, meaning that when it comes to knowing when someone is lying, typically we don't. Could it be that we don't want to know? So researchers speculate. Because it turns out that humans are actually terrible judges of deception as a rule, and the cues that we typically rely on to judge truthfulness or lying—faulty eye contact, nervous twitches, vocal hesitation—are, for the most part, totally unrelated to actual honesty. Even though people consistently report extremely high levels of self-confidence in their abilities to detect deception, and even though our judicial system hinges on the supposed accuracy of face-to-face judgments, the success rate among even those trained to sniff out lies isn't much better than 50 percent—that is, no better than random guessing. Frustrated deception researchers have been forced to conclude that humans just aren't sufficiently motivated to detect deception, and may even have a bias against knowing the truth, out of self-protection. Successful deception-detection would clearly be maladaptive when it comes to sustaining relationships. Unsuccessful deception-detection turns out to be the wiser strategy, a hedge against the loneliness and isolation that might result from successfully detecting the lies of friends and intimates on a regular basis. In short, we would not be mistaken in regarding any instance of successful deception as a complex interpersonal pact between liar and lied-to not to know the truth.

Yet even if a certain amount of deception is a given in social life, even if deception-detection goes against all our best interests, the sustaining premise of modern coupled life is that our intimates are those we *don't* lie to: we like to think of intimacy as a private enclave of authenticity set apart from ordinary social falseness and superficialities. The general view is that when truth-telling fails, so has the relationship. Or at least the majority of Americans express such beliefs when queried: recall that this was a rather incessant topic of punditry, polling, and water-cooler conversation throughout the Clinton years. (The question of why Hillary Clinton didn't just decamp the Clinton marriage when faced with Bill's chronic lies was frequently asked, and it was often regarded as a sign of her own moral failings that she didn't—out-of-control ambition was the usual culprit cited.) According to the tenets of this intimacy paradigm, adultery's crimes are not confined to adulterating monogamy—even worse, it adulterates the honesty that presumably obtained prior to adultery's ruinous arrival on the scene.

There's no doubt that catching a mate in a deception is

injurious for anyone who holds that transparency is the sine qua non of intimacy, and most of us do. It's typical to feel that having been deceived means having been disrespected, even humiliated. The irony—if we dare call it that—is that the rationale for deception is generally to *avoid* hurting people. Some calculation has been made "at some level" (once again, sustained self-reflection on the subject can prove daunting) that the truth will put something or someone at risk; deception thus may come to seem like the lesser-evil path when finding oneself in a sticky double bind: those occasions when opposing things are demanded of us, or desired by us, such as when society (or a mate) demands one thing, inner life another. But wanting two things at once is, after all, the topography of the Freudian psyche. We're split selves: ego one moment, id the next; or more to the point, both at once, afflicted with fantasies and wishes that never entirely succumb to the reality principle, no matter how much they're beaten into submission by socialization and its internal thugs, guilt and self-punishment. Having more than one desire may be modern intimacy's biggest taboo, but cramming the entirety of a libido into those tight domestic confines and acquiescing to a world of pre-shrunk desires is, for some, also *self-betrayal,* in the fullest—that is, the most split and unreconciled—sense of the word "self."

And hence, couple deception. No, it's not pretty. No one particularly admires a liar; likely no one particularly aspires to be one. But what does lying to intimates mean but that some hapless individual's emotions have fallen out of step with institutional dictates, that desires haven't fallen automatically into line like little gooselings? Though could it be a false premise that they invariably do? Geese are one thing, humans with our messy subjectivities another. A more accurate description of the situation might be that we've mortgaged our emotional well-being to intimacy institutions that hinge on elaborate fictions themselves, at least to the extent that feelings are unpredictable, that desires aren't always coherent or static, that knowing what you want in the realm of love and intimacy isn't an exact science, and people do occasionally change. You can't legally or morally contract to uphold a contract based on false premises. If the conventions we're pledged to sustain aren't permanently sustainable—or not always, and not for everyone, despite insisting on a no-questions-asked commitment to them—well, who's being deceptive?

Unfortunately for everyone involved, the deceptions of personal life aren't merely endemic, they're ricocheting off the walls. We may love to espouse the virtues of truth and transparency, but truthfully, *is* this what anyone really wants? Or is what we actually want truth under the right circumstances—meaning palatable truths, truths that put nothing at risk: namely our emotions, our real estate holdings, and in the case of coupled life, the assurance that "things" are working and that two deeply split and not entirely self-knowing individuals are in affective and sexual concordance (including over thorny and not always predictable issues like sexual exclusivity)? Is "truth" what we're after, or is it for a partner to adhere to all the desire and movement restrictions necessary for our own emotional well-being to be assured? (Just for the record, these aren't identical.)

Unhappily, the mate plays a dual role in this deception-riddled state of affairs: on the one hand a potential injured party, on the other the local enforcement wing for a deceptive institution. (And perhaps even betrayer-in-turn.) Yes, exposing a partner in a lie *is* an emotional auto wreck. One hopes the survivors will limp away, but no doubt some will end up crippled and scarred. Driving by these scenes of horror you cringe and avert your gaze, knowing that it happens all the time even as you hope it won't happen to you; but with that many tons of potential destruction rushing around at any one moment, a certain percentage of it is going to collide. (Though do you ever find yourself wondering—maybe just a bit uncharitably—if some of these victims may have courted their fates: speeding on blind curves, being overconfident, taking too much for granted?)* It's all so horrifying, yet also completely ordinary—until it happens to you, of course. But private transport comes with an automatic death toll; as we know, it's built into the system. So it is with our pothole-ridden intimacy systems, especially to the extent that they refuse to acknowledge their own contradictions and feign oblivion instead, causing so much damage just to sustain their own self-deceptions. The rest of us are left bearing the emotional brunt, and entirely to protect a self-regarding institution from the narcissistic injury of admitting its fundamental category error: the error of assuming that individual desires and social necessities automatically replicate each other. Or in the event that they

---

*Yes, there can also be a degree of emotional game playing involved in these scenes, these funny little couple rituals. To wit: does anyone "get caught" who hasn't to some degree courted it? Conversely, given how unskilled we apparently all are at detecting deception, you'd clearly have to be rather a devotee of detection to find anything out in the first place. Do such pairs attract? Does every deceiving spouse find her special prosecutor; every liar his designated detector?

don't, that desires tempted astray can be wrenched back into formation by exercises of will and renunciation. The question "What if they're not?" will simply not be discussed: that's your problem.

Which brings us back to . . . your problem. As anyone who's ever taken up one of the available roles in the adultery plot knows, the question of the future will at some point present itself. Will this thing end, and how? Who will fare well, and who badly? Which alliances will be left standing, which will be "history?" Clearly the specter of change is as enticing as it is petrifying. But before you get any rash ideas about truth-telling, or tunneling for freedom and making a run for it, remember that armed guards—children, public opinion, superegos—patrol the perimeters, and the attack dogs are starved for scandal. The next chewed-up social exile, hated by friends and family, causing hurt to everyone merely to satisfy craven selfish urges for happiness—yes, that despicable sorry friendless figure could be you.

Some affairs don't end, and manage to go on for years, even evolving into auxiliary marriages. (Tony Tanner notes of Emma Bovary that it's quite possible to rediscover in adultery all the banality of marriage—though must we think this inevitable?) Some affairs end well, fading into mutual fond memories or friendships—a gradual waning of passion over time can achieve this denouement. (A gradual *mutual* waning is the key element in this equation: no one likes feeling discarded while still libidinally engaged.) Some affairs will go on to become primary couples in their own right: old partnerships are dissolved, new ones formed. (Likely with all the usual domestic couple "issues" and interdictions: second, third, or fourth marriages don't necessarily revamp the couple form; usually they just serialize it.)

But love affairs *can* feel utterly transforming, and how few opportunities there are to feel that way in normal life, which by definition militates against transformation. You get to surrender to emotions you forgot you could have: to desire and to being desired (how overwhelming *that* can feel when it's been a while), and the thrill of the new thing, of course, but what really keeps you glued to the phone till all hours of the night—conversations sparkling with soulfulness and depth you hadn't known you possessed, exchanging those searching whispered intimacies—is a very different new love-object: *yourself.* The new beloved mirrors this fascinating new self back to you, and admit it, you're madly in love with both of them.

So here you are, temporarily transformed, madly enamored, terribly confused, on the cusp of . . . something. Either you hadn't realized how unhappy you were, or you knew exactly how unhappy you were, or that wasn't the issue— but however it started, whether it's the first time or just the most recent time, let's say things have now gotten a lot more . . . *unexpectedly complicated* than you'd anticipated. You're in love, you're beside yourself, your life feels like it's falling apart, you need to *think,* but thinking is not exactly your forte at the moment. Something has to give. Maybe that wonderfully understanding lover has suddenly started making demands or invoking previously declared timetables, or reminding you of various rash statements and implied (or explicit) promises, or has taken to issuing psychological assessments with a little too much truth to them (after all, between the confessions and the post-coital intimacies, this person knows you pretty darn well by now), or chosen to mistake "I love you's" and "what if's"—the semantics of everyday misery, as everyone knows, or should—for the language of a real future, and is calling in the chips? (Admittedly they can sound similar, and restless adulterers, like moldering POWs, will generally say anything for a shot at freedom.) *"But you said . . ."* the lover will say—as if you hadn't also said all along you didn't have a clue what you were doing. *"I meant it when I said it!"* you'll find yourself protesting, not really liking the sound of it. Or, *"I never meant to hurt anyone,"* which sounds a little feeble too.

No, not everyone will manage the graceful ending—or even a graceful continuation—under such circumstances, with so many contradictions and aporias and deceptions bouncing off the walls of such confined quarters, and saddled with the ever-flawed state of self-knowledge that is our sorry lot. Note that this is a time for *extreme caution!* Disastrous fast-moving storm fronts may be headed in your direction: the winds are whipping around ominously, a lawn chair is hurled across the yard, a power line comes down, and things are starting to look calamitous—in your own psyche, that is. Yes, under barometric conditions such as these, bad things have a way of happening to nice people, unpleasant things, for instance, "unplanned discoveries"— hardly an unknown occurrence at exactly such moments. Unaccountably, a letter is left out, a phone call overheard, an e-mail misaddressed, an appointment missed, the mate makes an inquiring call, and you're not where you were meant to be, and . . .

How could this have happened? Life is suddenly wall-to-wall pain and confusion. Yelling, tears, ultimatums; domestic life is in chaos. You don't know *what* to do. Agonized conversations with the lover; angry or tearful or bitter conversations with the mate; emergency sessions with therapists; rambling repetitive conversations with any friends willing to endure the crisis with you.

Here's a suggestion: why not try contrition? *"I never meant to hurt you. I feel like shit."* If you can pull it off, this *may* work with both spouse and lover. Of course it also may not work: neither may be as sympathetic to your dilemma as you would like. In which case you can try standing your ground: "Look how unhappy *I've* been. Look what I've been *driven to*!"

If the mate is willing to saddle some of the blame, renouncing an affair may be just the recommitment gesture needed for a "fresh start." And maybe things will actually improve. The mate vows to become more attentive, or less critical, or more sexually adventurous. You both make pledges to *work harder* at the relationship. Marriage counselors are consulted; plans for vacations or domestic improvements are undertaken; real estate purchases are considered: all capital investments in relationship continuation. (Perhaps the thought has even started fluttering around unbidden, somewhere back in the old reptile brain, that being found out wasn't an *entirely* bad way to ameliorate domestic conditions?)

Though needless to say, once you've been caught in an affair, domestic life quickly transforms itself into the domestic equivalent of a South American police state, subjecting you to periodic search and seizures, ritual interrogations

134

about movements and associations. Independent documentation may be demanded. Desk drawers are rifled for clues, bills audited for improprieties, and so-called friends transform themselves into a network of informants as extensive as former Stasi agents. A Baltimore therapist recommends that couples who survive infidelity episodes create a "family fund" that the betrayed spouse can use to hire a private detective to ensure future fidelity. (Obviously any future affairs are going to necessitate the cunning and sustained duplicity of an Anthony Blunt.)* But you've learned your lesson—you'll never be ambivalent again, right? It may be a few years before you're let out of the house alone, but it's really good to be back home. (Unfortunately, that new self you'd met and fallen in love with during your affair has probably started seeming like a distant acquaintance or someone encountered in a fugue state; the lover, to whom you so recently pledged body and soul . . . well it's all too painful to think about. So you don't, aside from the occasional stabbing pangs of longing, and the dark gaping sinkhole where that exciting feeling of aliveness once was—and the frankness and the great sex and all that fun—but you know you've done the right thing even if you feel vaguely like a shit, and even if self-reflection is not something you feel much like chancing these days, if ever again.)

Some may choose the confession route in lieu of exposure, though "choose" may not be precisely the right word in all cases, because you may have just woken up in the

---

*For our post–Cold War readers: the notorious "fourth man." A Soviet spy so well concealed that he was actually knighted by Queen Elizabeth.

middle of the night and blurted it out, or an innocent question of the mate's like "How was your day?" prompts an entirely unplanned tell-all—*"There's something I have to tell you"*—or a too-pointed joke or question from out of the blue ("Are you having an affair with————?") catches you off guard and your expression says it all. Or maybe you haven't yet been exposed or confessed or caught off guard, but mounting guilt and conflict are gnawing at your insides because it really *is* serious, and you're finding that you can't go on leading dual love lives and performing the complicated emotional balancing acts it requires, or at least various somatic symptoms are issuing uncomfortable warnings to that effect. Or you're *really* fucking up at work, or you've been spotted somewhere, causing panic and internal disarray, and basically you're starting to realize that something has to give.

However it happened, whatever the particulars, let's say you're at a crossroads. Choices are before you, big, threatening life-altering choices. Stay or go? End things or continue? But *which* things? Try to hold onto those wonderful feelings of elation and transformation, the thrill of possibility and that enticing new self you've been so enamored by? And "pay the price"—not even knowing exactly what that will be? Or opt for maturity and stability, and a retreat back into the very life that you've been recently plotting those elaborate escapes from, the one that's felt dead and depressing for longer than you care to admit. Big, imponderable, painful questions plague your days and haunt your sleepless nights. Who are you? What are you allowed to want from life? Is risk worth the risk? Why is change so impossible? Can you even contemplate giving up your discontent, or is

it such a familiar old friend that you feel legible to yourself
only in its company?

You have no answers; you've never been so miserable.

When possibilities for altering life conditions do very occasionally force themselves into daylight like tiny, delicate
sprouts struggling up through the hard dirt, what an array
of sharp-bladed mechanisms stand ready to mow them into
mulch before they manage to take root! The story of why
things don't change is a long and complicated story indeed.
("Things" may be taken to mean domestic arrangements,
or selves, or social structures themselves, given their mutually reinforcing aspects.) When it comes to domestic life,
every unhappy couple member moonlights as a CPA, expert
in cost-benefit calculations, armed with a private formula
to assess the trade-offs, risks, past investments, and future
payoffs of bad emotional bargains. Divide your current
unhappiness by how well you'd come out in the property
settlement, multiply by some private floating variable—
guilt, fear of the unknown, how to explain it to the kids if
there are kids (to relatives and friends, if not)—and what
you arrive at is a misery quotient: a precise calibration of how
much emotional rigor mortis you can tolerate in exchange
for a sense of stability.

Certainly there aren't any guarantees in the transformation
business. But neither is chronic unhappiness a particularly
fertile soil for producing the resilience required to transform
much of anything, even in limited and local ways. (Partner
changes may feel momentous, but are actually rather local
in the big scheme of things.) Likewise, low-level depression

and habituated self-hate may be the by-products of coupled unhappiness, but they're also the internal conditions that propel us into these emotional bargains in the first place, and keep us committed to them so tenaciously. Yes, the escape routes are well-trodden—love affairs, "mid-life crises"— but also strewn with the left-behind luggage and abandoned promises of the faint-of-heart, who encountered unforeseen obstacles—panic, guilt, self-engineered exposures—along the way and were forced to turn back. (On the generational repetitions of coupled unhappiness, on *not deserving more* as a heritable trait, please read on.)

No wonder combustible combinations of sex and romance so often stand in for knowing what you're doing. The discontented classes are creative geniuses at inventing ways to have transformational longings and desires without actual cognition, cobbling together illicit ragtag assemblages out of scraps of stolen moments and filched emotions, taking up residence in them in starving, greedy ways like tourists in the world of gratification armed with temporary visas. But thinking about it does rock boats: the path from self-awareness to court-ordered property settlements is a slippery slope, and don't think that every social being with a bank account doesn't know it. Thus the spontaneous uprising *("I didn't mean for this to happen!"),* and getting caught in the tsunami of the moment *("I never thought things would get this serious!").* Of course when it comes to consciousness, bodily sensations often do precede conscious analysis (just as Marx observed long ago about the consciousness of overwork): you notice that you feel shitty and start to wonder why. Or more likely, somehow just can't figure it out.

These impeded relations between feeling and thinking, that abyss between bodily desires and self-knowledge—they're what keep the shrinks in business. But despite the privatizing languages of therapy, these aren't only private life dilemmas, they're also collective ones, and with analogous social dimensions. There were wildcat strikes long before there was a labor movement; "acting out" has preceded self-awareness throughout history. If the spontaneous uprising is a proto-political form, the historical inference is that where collective awareness is impeded, it's because some entrenched interest would be put at risk were those impediments lifted—and by any changes to business-as-usual that such awareness might lead to. All available resources will thus be marshaled to prevent such occurrences, and these take ever-more subtle forms: not a soldier on every corner, but conscripting our ways of seeing the world, including basic "common sense" and conventional wisdom, and even all the reassuring clichés we all turn to in times of uncertainty, like when enticing possibilities for change appear on the horizon sending you into a state of panic.

Here's a reassuring cliché: *"For the sake of the children."* Yes, don't forget there are children to think about, or often there are. Investing any residue utopianism or transformational desires in kids is one kind of answer, and of course the socially sanctioned one. "For the sake of the children": end of discussion. What a noble sacrifice; virtue is in your court. Though needless to say, "for the sake of the children" is rather a selective enterprise, holding sway far more frequently when it comes to guilty matters like divorce than when it comes to pocketbook issues like education spending (America ranks fourteenth in per capita dollars spent on education out of fifteen industrialized countries). Or when it comes to every other form of childhood health and well-being: the U.S. ranks twenty-eighth in infant mortality rates, which means behind virtually every other industrialized nation in the world—and one in five of the surviving American kids lives in poverty. Sentimentality about children's welfare comes and goes apparently: highest when there's the chance to moralize about adult behavior, lowest when it comes to resource allocation. Of course, all sorts of dollars are available to be thrown into expensive longitudinal studies gauging the effects of divorce on children, studies whose results invariably mirror the views of the principal researcher: conservatives will discover that divorce is disastrous, liberals will discover that children are resilient. But if women's post-divorce income drops an average of 30 percent, if the single parent household is a predictor of poverty, it turns out that cushioning children from the economic consequences of divorce or single parenthood is a simple matter of formulating social policy that conforms to the reality of the lives of the citizenry instead of moralizing at them. As Sweden's system of guaranteed child allocations proves with its childhood poverty rate of under 3 percent compared with 22 percent with our preferred method—which is to ignore reality, let everyone fend for themselves, and blame the consequences on lax morals or not working hard enough—whether at marriage or the minimum wage jobs that produce the poverty in the first place.

To those who want to maintain that non-divorced families turn out less neurotic or happier adults, the evidence supporting such views is a little scanty: please look around. Are traditional families really such happy, neurosis-free places? They seem to produce their share of criminals and socio-paths, and run-of-the-mill unhappiness. Clearly the answer to the much-debated question "Does divorce harm children?" should be "Compared to what?" Compared to contexts of chronic unhappiness and dissatisfaction, to unmet needs as status quo, to bitching mothers, remote fathers, and other gendered forms of quotidian misery? Is it really likely that the majority of unhappy parents are also such master thespians that kids remain unaffected by family contexts of emotional distance or sexual coldness or mutual disrespect or long-term disappointment? Unfortunately what "for the sake of the children" really means is multi-generational training grounds for lowered expectations as an affective norm; for "that's just the way it is" as a guide to living; for the idea that change spells catastrophe and trauma, and wanting anything more or different is ridiculous.

It's also too bad if presenting false images of your own emotional state seems like the only way to have the authenticity you want with your kids (or another instance of the everyday deceptions required to sustain normal life). Note that the emotional costs of those trade-offs are transmitted in subtle ways in family contexts: in the most mundane everyday interactions and even through body language, not just in the big life lessons; note too that inherited shame is not a particularly enabling mode of being-in-the-world. Though no doubt if you've grown up in such a place yourself, it feels like home. Sadly for all of us born into these kinds of households and deceptions and social forms, happiness *is* likely to be a fleeting experience: "stolen moments," compensatory forms, renounced pleasures. But in the land of lowered expectations, what more do you deserve? You couldn't "live with yourself" if you gave it up—though of course you haven't really had the emotional experience of anything else, so how would you know? And most likely neither will the kids.

Chapter Four

... AND THE PURSUIT
OF HAPPINESS

"In the '90s, Infidelity Sparks More Outrage Than It Did a Few Decades Ago!" a *Newsweek* cover trumpeted in a mid-decade story. But adultery was more than a personal dilemma in pre-millennial America, it had become a major political issue, nearly bringing down a president, felling two House Speakers (including Newt Gingrich, the supposed paragon of sexual morality behind the "family values" rhetoric simultaneously blanketing the country), staining the credentials of Cabinet members and assorted politicians—one, in a promising bid for gender equity, a congress*woman* (Representative Helen Chenoweth of Idaho who had strenuously called for Bill Clinton's resignation given his extramarital affair, and despite her own long-term affair with a married man)—ending the careers of a few multi-starred generals, derailing the nomination of a chairman of the Joint Chiefs of Staff who was compelled to withdraw from consideration amid revelations of an affair well over a decade before, and making a national laughingstock of a high-profile presidential consultant (Dick Morris, outed as an aficionado of toe sucking and call girls—more on this to come). Seemingly upstanding and loudly "pro-family" Republican national emblems were exposed hounding after furtive nonfamilial pleasures, often while clamoring for presidential impeachment for similar activities. Representative Henry Hyde, who led the Clinton impeachment committee, was forced to admit to a five-year affair with a married woman ("The statute of limitations has long since passed on my youthful indiscretions" was his response; Hyde was forty-six when the affair ended). Representative Dan Burton turned out to have fathered a child in an extramarital affair (somehow neglected in the campaign literature when the rest of the family were trotted out for photo-ops); Burton had led the campaign fund-raising investigation of Clinton initiated by Clinton-haters as a chaser to the sexual investigations.

A terrible disease named Desire was sweeping the Beltway and no one knew who would be its next victim. Political candidates nervously proclaimed marital fidelity before a skeptical electorate, or preemptively confessed past marital troubles now miraculously healed, dutiful sedated-appearing spouses in tow, and often just one step ahead of tabloid reporters offering large bounties of cash to any former lovers willing to spill their stories. Others were obliged to drop out of politics altogether if those options proved, for whatever reasons, unfeasible. Retaining the goodwill of former flingmates was now a prerequisite for elected office, a skill never previously considered worth acquiring among the politician demimonde. *Hustler* magazine publisher and longtime political provocateur Larry Flynt took out a full-page ad in the *Washington Post* offering a million dollars to any lovers of elected officials or high-level officeholders who could prove it and would go public; impending Flynt-generated revelations led to the surprise resignation of designated house speaker Bob Livingstone, who stunned his colleagues by confessing from the House floor that he had "on occasion strayed from my marriage," but had sought spiritual counseling and been forgiven by his wife. (Because Livingstone resigned prior to *Hustler*'s print date and the story broke in the national news instead, Flynt refused to fork over the promised million to the tell-all ex.) Another of the anti-Clintonites outed as an adulterer was Georgia congressman Bob Barr, whose second wife reported that Barr—or the "the twice-divorced family-values cheerleader," in Flynt's characterization—was having an affair with his soon-to-be third wife when he announced to the second, shortly before Thanksgiving, that he was leaving her and their two sons, ages five and a half and four.*

The public/private distinction in American political culture was eroding faster than the California coastline or the value of technology stocks; the rules were changing, and no one knew where it was going to stop. Unthinkably, the pornography industry had infiltrated the political process and actually shifted the course of national history: Livingstone, effectively unseated by Flynt, would have been third in line for the presidency. Pundits bemoaned the decline of civility, op-ed think pieces intoned highmindedly about privacy incursions. Still, wasn't there also something secretly

---

*Among other revelations was that Barr, a staunch antiabortion crusader, had paid for his wife to have an abortion during their marriage. In his public incarnation, Barr was prone to statements like this: "The very foundations of our society are in danger of being burned. The flames of hedonism, the flames of narcissism, the flames of self-centered morality are licking at the very foundations of our society: the family unit." (Despite his professed concern for the family unit, Barr's ex-wife appears to be rather bitter about the treatment she received within hers.)

gratifying about nabbing so many national leaders with their pants—and their contradictions—around their ankles?

But why exactly had adultery suddenly become a *federal case,* now the favored metaphor for all broken promises, national or personal? Why was it no longer a private enterprise or a tacitly accepted privilege of office, but a new form of national malaise? Note that the family values theme achieved ascendancy in political rhetoric at precisely the same moment. We were a nation divided: our national leaders a bunch of split personalities flip-flopping between public sanctimony and private debauches; an electorate split between wanting to believe them and wanting to expose them. There was an "as if" quality to national politics: voters acting as if the political rhetoric were believable; as if they were shocked, shocked by each successive scandal. As if they'd never heard about JFK and Marilyn Monroe, or LBJ, or FDR, or Ike, or any other philandering politician.

But the American nation itself is rather a split personality case, historically speaking, with one leg in that founding Puritanism still lodged deep at the core of the national sensibility and still periodically burping to the surface in gassy fits of censoriousness and prohibition; the other planted in a collective spirit of adventurism and experimentalism, still commemorating revolutionaries, pioneers, explorers, inventor-entrepreneurs, and anti-bureaucratic loner-rebels as national character types and founders. Isn't our entire national history a seesaw of emancipation movements alternating with repression movements, as if we couldn't make up our minds? Interestingly—perhaps in consequence?—some big national ruckus over sex or marriage is periodically elected as the chosen venue for these foundational splits to once more play themselves out. With sex and marriage already such conflicted venues, why should this be surprising—when anxieties about "the state of the union" arise, where better to enact them?

The narrative hook for the latest episode of this conflicted tale was the private lives of politicians. The backstory: a post-sexual-revolution-family-values triumphalism battling it out with the last residues of boomer sex liberationism along with its "pleasure now" credo, each side trying to beat the other to a bloody pulp like Unionists and Confederates at Sharpsburg. The twist was that it wasn't merely two opposing factions this time; in more than a few cases we got to watch these warring tendencies embodied in one person, more often than not some prominent national figure. Words like "compartmentalization" entered the political vocabulary, and a long decade of national psychodrama ensued. An ill-prepared nation was forced to play psychoanalyst and hoist its conflicted leaders onto the couch, there to ponder that thorniest of psychological quandaries: Does anyone "get caught" who doesn't "at some level" self-engineer this fate? The moralizer cum secret libertine, the randy evangelist—these too are longstanding national character types revivified for the '90s (and obviously known to us *as* types only to the extent that they haven't successfully maintained their facades—perhaps have even courted exposure). If one of the less functional aspects of the split personality is disavowal—one side needs to disavow knowing what the other side is up to—disavowal does closely resemble hypocrisy when exposed, which invariably it is. (Though political hypocrisy may be endemic, it's also supposed to be a secret: exposing it risks shaking up the whole business of liberal governance and its fundamental presumption that the citizenry actually consents to these arrangements.)*

The scandal factor did make the normally turgid business of electoral politics unexpectedly interesting in this period, teetering as it did between civic soap opera and a nationwide philosophical seminar on the antinomies of desire and marriage or the travails of long-term love: Plato's *Symposium* rewritten for mass society and debated in the daily headlines, thankfully replacing the usual soporific policy issues and economic indicators. The electorate, polled for our feelings on a moment-by-moment basis, were variously contemptuous, pained, and occasionally infuriated, as we dutifully reported. Many did seem to be taking it all quite personally, as if *we* were the ones being dallied with, and the airwaves hummed with moral outrage. Clearly, for some, these matters cut a little too close to home. After all, these cheating politicians were our *representatives*. These adulterous generals were our nation's *defense*. These were our deputies, our stand-ins. They were Main Street U.S.A., they were the face of America, they were *us*. Which also meant they had to pay, and pay big, since none of us was going to admit it.

But it wasn't only extramarital activities occupying the attention of the politician classes, the entire political sphere

---

*Regarding hypocrisy: with a $9 billion recession-proof national pornography industry, we do have to assume at least some degree of overlap between pornography's customer base and the family values political base—though try finding anyone willing to admit to that either.

had become obsessed with the problem of marriage itself. Public policy debates were preoccupied with salvaging what had come to be seen as a battered institution, in turn dictating decision-making about everything from welfare policy to tax reform to sex education funding, even spearheading a movement to revise the Constitution itself. With a 50 percent divorce rate now established as a permanent feature of the socio-personal landscape, 30 percent higher than in 1970 (and an overall rate closer to 70 percent in the Pacific states, which tend to lead the nation as trendsetters); and census figures revealing a precipitous drop in the overall number of married couples as well as of traditional nuclear families; and a 1999 Rutgers University study reporting that a mere 38 percent of Americans who are married describe themselves as actually happy in that state, the only population now unreservedly enthusiastic about marriage were homosexuals, for whom the right to legally marry had emerged as a key political goal, AIDS having forced an early demise of the gay activism of previous decades, which once battled the vanilla norms of heterosexual coupledom (or in queer theory's jargon, "heteronormativity") instead of trying to replicate them.

If heterosexuals were bailing out of matrimony in droves, at least there was another group standing by to repopulate the ranks, like a new wave of civic-minded immigrants eager to move in and spruce up abandoned neighborhoods with fresh coats of paint and small business loans: soon it becomes the hip place to be and the middle classes all want to move back in. Unfortunately not everyone saw it that way: when a circuit court in Hawaii ordered the state to issue same-sex marriage licenses because not doing so was discriminatory, Congress was suddenly awash in matrimonial enthusiasm. Despite the fact that the Hawaii ruling was shortly overturned by a higher court, Congress pushed through the so-called Defense of Marriage Act (DOMA), a custom-built stockade fence to protect matrimony against infiltration by nefarious homosexual elements and safeguard the more panicky states from having to recognize another state's gay marriages, should any state actually grant the privilege, which none had. (Vermont would later grant gays the far more limited right to apply for civil union status, but to date, no state permits gays to actually marry.) DOMA's supporters argued that traditional heterosexual marriage was the "fundamental building block of our society," even while—in the case of family values champion and then–House Speaker Gingrich—conducting a semi-open extramarital affair that would soon end his own heterosexual marriage (and political career).* The bill was quickly signed into law by Bill Clinton, another noted marital enthusiast, and publicly endorsed by First Lady Hillary Clinton, for whom heterosexual coupledom had also not been entirely unproblematic. Or so one may speculate, given her designated role as cuckoldess in the most highly scrutinized marital dalliance in American history. In one of her few public com-

---

*Gingrich, who had spearheaded the so-called Republican Revolution and whose rhetoric hinged on promoting family fidelity and sexual conservatism, resigned his congressional seat and speakership in the midst of rumors of an affair with a congressional aide, rumors which were confirmed by testimony at his subsequent divorce trial. This was, in fact, his second divorce; reports were that he had initiated his first by presenting his then-wife with a handwritten settlement agreement while she was in the hospital recovering from uterine cancer surgery.

ments on the subject, Mrs. Clinton did say—though this was much later, during her subsequent New York Senate campaign—that the country's leaders should "start talking about the importance of marriage," adding, "Marriages are hard. They are hard work. I'd be the first to tell you." (The rhetoric of the factory proves its utility once again.) Infuriated, gay activists retaliated to the passage of DOMA by outing a round of gay Republicans who'd voted to preserve marriage for heterosexuality, although one, Jim Kolbe of Arizona, outsmarted them by preemptively outing himself.

Obviously marriage needed defending, but was it from gay weddings or from its own disaffected habitués? No, it could only be lesbians picking out silver patterns and gay men marching down the aisle to the strains of Pachelbel's *Canon* driving all those otherwise contented heterosexuals to Divorce Court. Following DOMA's passage, over half the states passed additional completely redundant definition-of-marriage laws, exactly reproducing DOMA, including California's Proposition 22, known as the Knight Initiative, in honor of the state senator who sponsored it. It happened that Knight's own son was openly gay, publicly supported gay marriage, and was in a long-term relationship himself. An organization based in Washington, D.C., named the Alliance for Marriage, began lobbying for a constitutional amendment that would also reiterate DOMA. Clearly if this could pass, heterosexual marriage would finally triumph once more, having driven so many sharp legislative stakes through the foul hearts of its gay terrorizers. Be on the lookout for divorce rates to plummet shortly after.

In the meantime, let's try a brief thought experiment: let's contemplate possible congressional responses to the gay marriage question in some imaginary land where political discourse had even a tenuous relation to the lived reality of the nation's inhabitants. For instance, what if, in place of pointless legislation, our representatives had been able to acknowledge that the issue affected them personally on various levels—for some, raising questions about their own sexuality, for others, about their own well-publicized difficulties negotiating those occasionally thorny matrimonial thickets (that damn fidelity business), and perhaps in the process initiating a nationwide process of reflection on the difficulties and merits of the marital enterprise itself, which, after all, the rest of us grapple with ourselves. There could have been hearings, expert witnesses—an actual civic dialogue of the sort Mrs. Clinton endorsed. Creative conservatives might even have managed to find politically pragmatic reasons to support gay marriage initiatives: here could be a way of tempering those more outré homosexual tendencies to the scale of hetero proprieties. Who knows what transformative effects marriage licenses might have?*

Any of these would be politically imaginative responses (thus politically unimaginable ones). If only they didn't demand actual honesty about the politics of marriage. If only they didn't require a modicum of self-reflection on the part of our elected officials about the substantial degree of contradiction they and their fellow members were them-

---

*From a different vantage point, this would be an argument against gay marriage. So Michael Warner contends in *The Trouble With Normal,* which staged a debate over the issue with conservative gay journalist Andrew Sullivan, who had previously made the pro–gay marriage case in *Virtually Normal: An Argument about Homosexuality.*

selves publicly enacting around the subject of marriage. If only it didn't mean giving up scapegoating the one group least engaged by far in endangering marriage, and acknowledging that, whatever was endangering marriage, it was located a lot closer to home (their own backyards, for instance)—it wasn't gays wanting the right to visit each other in the hospital or get onto each other's insurance policies. Clearly, this was impossible. Instead marriage was elected the new disease of the week: everyone hunting for a miracle cure and shedding public crocodile tears for an institution about which ambivalence is—if the private behavior of our own representatives counts for anything—endemic. Keep gays out. Keep heterosexuals in, with electrified fences if necessary.

Meanwhile, researchers at academic institutes, like the Rutgers University Marriage Project, were producing complicated longitudinal studies "to track, predict, and reverse" the patterns of marital dissatisfaction they were uncovering. "Knowing the pattern of marriage relationships might help couples stay together, if they can come up with positive ways to cope with it," as one researcher put it hopefully, trying to mitigate the grim conclusions his own study had produced. "Marriage is now, as it has always been, hard work. . . . There is no obvious course to follow, so couples just have to keep working," said another, predictably. (Once again, the word "marriage" can scarcely be uttered without the language of the salt mine in its wake.) Conservative think tanks like the Institute for American Values issued what were billed as "nonpartisan" reports suggesting an end to no-fault divorce, as a way of "strengthening civil society" and "improving the quality of marriage." How preventing divorce would improve marriages and not just further the unhappiness of the unhappily married remained unspecified.

What this so-called crisis in marriage *meant* or why the populace and its elected representatives were fleeing its purported delights in record numbers were not permissible questions. The possibility that marriage was an institution in transition or an institution being redefined rather than one in need of life support could not be entertained. Nor could the possibility that these transitions in the family structure respond to larger—even global—economic shifts rather than deriving from individual irresponsibility: perhaps a postindustrial economy *produces* a post-nuclear family.*
The option of accommodating such transitions in relevant policy decisions was also not worth considering; the problem was individual malfeasants—the divorced, the unwed (particularly those rash enough to procreate), and of course homosexuals—all of whom had failed to uphold social expectations and were causing an innocent institution pain and suffering. Politicians even managed to blame *poverty* on high divorce rates (because it couldn't be the other way around). If one in three divorces propels a family below the poverty line, the only solution was to force individuals to stay in unhappy marriages.

---

*One conservative political theorist, Francis Fukuyama, did actually take this stand. His version is that the shift from an industrial to an information economy (one in which brains are more of an employment asset than brawn) opened career opportunities to women because there was a need to draw from a larger labor pool; this in turn weakened the nuclear family. Feminism itself was merely a by-product, says Fukuyama, an epiphenomenon of changes in macroeconomic conditions.

Despite the rampant illogic, a guilty, emotionally beaten-down citizenry might have bought the message, except for the buzz of cognitive dissonance that overtook the national sensibility as one after another of these same pontificators became subjects of tabloid exposés, in which altogether different pictures of contemporary marriage emerged, like tiny glistening kernels of reality inside bubbles of punctured hypocrisy, and in which, as we saw, even the most vocal "pro-family" politicos were themselves unable to conform to the sexual and marital standards they were hawking to the rest of us.

If the most remarked-on trend in '90s national politics was the collapse of traditional distinctions between public and private spheres, if the private lives of public officials took on an intensified degree of collective meaning for the nation in this period, the Clinton impeachment trial was the logical and probably necessary culmination of these twin trends: a messy mud pie of three-ring circus and pro-jective identification, which is the name for the psychological syndrome in which split-off and disavowed parts of the self—particularly those regarded as bad—are projected onto someone else, there to become the target of aggression and hatred. (The playground wisdom "He who smelt it, dealt it" would be another way of expressing more or less the same thing.)

Even if *Time* magazine hadn't designated Bill Clinton the nation's "Libido in Chief," it was evident that this president had been elected to suffer for the sins of his countrymen, meaning the nation had chosen to elect a philandering hus-band—since there was no secret about it—and then perversely impaled him for it in a fit of ritualistic national bloodletting. And true to form—or to the logic of projective identification—it was demonstrably faithless Republican congressmen and congresswomen wielding the sharpest stakes, clamoring to claim their victim's entrails as a gruesome prize.

According to anthropologist Victor Turner, leaders often do emplot their lives as what he calls "social narratives," consciously or unconsciously acting in ways that allow them to become clothed with allusiveness and metaphor. The leader's body signifies the dilemmas of the nation, and we choose as our leaders those candidates who manage to make themselves legible to us as a collective mirror. But it's not only anthropologists who subscribe to this view or preliterate tribes alone who fetishize the chieftain's body: this is the essence of the modern political campaign. As one political consultant wrote, recounting the 1992 presidential election, "I put it to Clinton that launching a presidential candidacy was not unlike writing a novel: You had to create yourself as a sympathetic hero, in language that would touch a reader's heart and mind. Clinton readily agreed that he had so far failed to emerge as a rounded and credible character in the unfolding narrative of the election." In other words, "character," the political watchword of the decade, wasn't simply a synonym for conventional ethics or buttoned-up behavior. It also meant the ability of a particular political character to embody the right collective story for the moment. We citizens are choosy customers when it comes to our symbolic vehicles, refusing to hire those who fail to consummate their appointed narrative task, summarily firing the ones whose narratives have exhausted our inter-

est. Having the wrong narrative, even a mistimed one, registers as a failure of *charisma*. We find ourselves uncompelled.
Our imaginations aren't captured and we turn elsewhere,
seeking better stories and more enticing narrators.

Case in point: Republican presidential hopeful Bob Dole.
Throughout the 1996 presidential campaign, Candidate
Dole strove valiantly, but in the end fruitlessly, to make his
body signify a collective story to the electorate, straining to
make his war wounds and disabilities (a paralyzed arm and
hand) symbolize something about the nation's history and
future. If things had gone according to plan, his body would
have narrated a tale of triumph over adversity, stoicism in
the face of pain and injury, and sacrifice in the service of
American military hegemony. What Dole failed to realize
was that the nation was in the grips of an entirely different
story about itself, and that, for reasons yet to be ascer-
tained, the national narrative of the '90s was composed in
the idiom of sex, not sacrifice. Not receiving the message,
Dole kept invoking the "problem" of Clinton's character,
albeit by insisting he wouldn't bring it up (classy guy that he
was) while proceeding to do just that. Post-election reports
were that Dole dropped the character question very fast
after learning that the *Washington Post* was pursuing a
story about a four-year affair he'd had himself while married to his first wife, which though confirmed by the affair-
mate, the *Post* ultimately chose not to run. It might have
been better for him if they had. Dole's World War II–era
wounds seemed somehow old-fashioned and insignificant,
whereas Candidate Clinton's wounds—his embarrassing excesses, his blatant neediness, his fleshy welcoming thighs—

spoke to the nation, who loathed him, loved him, punished him, reelected him, and impeached him: in other words, were completely unable to take their eyes off him.*

All of this made it a strangely *theatrical* decade in America, one in which our elected representatives, as if under some strange form of collective autosuggestion, transformed themselves into amateur thespians and politics into a massive public theater project, impelled for reasons unknown to perform their marital dramas and dilemmas on the national proscenium. Clearly leadership styles vary throughout history and in different parts of the globe. Some leaders are showmen, some are buttoned-up bureaucrats, but a leader's body invariably condenses an array of meanings and messages, which may or may not entirely map onto political ideology—which may even complicate or contradict their official positions. Political theorist Robert Hariman calls it "political style": the repertoire of rhetorical conventions that leaders employ, consciously or unconsciously, and which guide how their constituents understand the signals they send, and color the meanings we attribute to actions and situations. Hariman provides four examples of different political styles, naming the politicians or political writers who best exemplify them: for the republican style, Cicero; for political realism, Machiavelli; for the courtly style, Haile Selassie; for the bureaucratic style, of course, Kafka. Other styles and figures quickly come to mind: for

---

*In his post-political career, Dole (still modeling himself as the anti-Clinton? Reenacting his political defeat in the sexual arena?) became a highly visible paid spokesman for Viagra, appearing in both print and TV ads.

populism, Peron; for paranoia, Nixon; and so on. The utility of political style is that it provides a sense of social cohesion; this would be why a leader's bodily symbols and symptoms become such indelible national emblems, as does a leader's spouse's body too—or wardrobe, or even accessories—recall that it was Imelda Marcos and her three thousand pairs of shoes that emblematized husband Ferdinand's corruption, not his monetary policies. (The shoe collection was put on public view after they fled the Philippines and was long the star attraction at the Malacanang Palace in Manila, until moved to a newly created "shoe museum" for permanent display.)

Certain political styles may also predominate in particular periods: times of national expansion would call for a different leadership style than times of belt-tightening. If politician marital sexuality became emblematic and hypervisible during the '90s, if it governed the way we understood the exercise of power and the national project itself, it could only mean that marital sexuality offered some way of condensing some other crucial set of meanings, thus becoming symbolically meaningful for the populace. If not, it would fail to signify: it would be non-emblematic. No one would pay attention. This was, we know, largely the state of things for the first few centuries of nationhood, when, notwithstanding the occasional jibe about a politician's private life or mistresses, the separate-spheres principle largely prevailed. The question of whether sexual behavior predicted political credibility or determined electability was not foremost on the national agenda; in millennial America, it seemed at times like the only political question worth discussing.

Apparently we were witnessing the birth of an entirely new political style: *spousal*. Would you want to be married to this politician?* It was the New Left that first popularized the phrase "the personal is the political," and the '90s witnessed its conservative revenant, with politician sexual behavior the litmus test in a new public theology around marriage. But it wasn't only conservatives or the religious right mounting the case. Marital politics came in all brands and sizes, with liberals and feminists weighing in too. In fact, women's opinions of political candidates were suddenly being treated with an altogether new seriousness across the spectrum, because after all, who is better equipped than *wives* to produce scathing insights about male spouses—this being the demographic from which our politicians are still typically drawn—or assess their bedability, or gauge their hidden faults?

Thus, women became the political oracles of spousal politics, and played the role to the hilt. Here, for instance, is feminist novelist Erica Jong on the op-ed page of the *New York Times:* "What do American women want in a president? The same thing we want in a husband." In electoral politics, according to Jong—author of *Fear of Flying,* the definitive '70s sexual liberation novel—women like a bit of the "bad boy" in their men; we're drawn to the ones who "unlock our passion in a way that defies reason." Thus

---

*Recall the classic line about Richard Nixon: "Would you buy a used car from this man?" If the main anxiety about the 1960s-era politician was that he was a shady salesman rather than a cheating spouse, it's evident that the trust issue is configured differently to suit the requirements of each political generation.

while women might have hated what Bill Clinton did, we couldn't bring ourselves to hate him completely, since he talked to us and even listened like "the communicative husband we'd always longed for." You could tell that a Jong-Clinton match would have had possibilities: she would have seen Bill as an interesting challenge, he would have appreciated *Fear of Flying*'s endorsement of guilt-free sexual experimentation. But not all the lady pundits were in such a forgiving mood. "I've been surprised by how profoundly this has shaken me," said a mother of two from McLean, Virginia, quoted in one of the *New York Times* daily roundups of women's views on Clinton. "I feel very shaken and betrayed on a personal level." Men were occasionally allowed to express their views if sufficiently spousal. A few years later, when New York mayor Rudolph Giuliani's extravagantly contentious divorce proceedings hit the national news, a forty-four-year-old Garden City man had this to say to the *Times*: "If he does this to his family, what will he do to the people?"

Connubial behavior was clearly the political question of the moment, and if by decade's end we were informed by those ubiquitous pollsters that the public had finally stopped caring about faithfulness, the issue still didn't just disappear. Instead we got the story of why politician fidelity *wasn't* an issue for the voting public. Rhetoricians have a name for this: "apophasis," which means the denial of the intent to speak of a subject, which in denying it, still speaks of it. Updated for mass media purposes, it would be the story about why X isn't a story, which continues to keep it alive *as* a story while disavowing any meaning to the subject.

Spousal politics also offered a new lens through which to

revamp national history and collective self-understanding. Conservative Marvin Olasky responded to the Clinton impeachment with *The American Leadership Tradition: Moral Vision from Washington to Clinton,* which argued—no surprise—that good husbands make good presidents, assessing how well previous national leaders managed to keep their lusts under control, from Revolutionary days to the present. Thus Thomas Jefferson, FDR, JFK (who "emphasized fast action, whether sexual or governmental"), and of course, Bill Clinton—skirt-chasers all—were leadership washouts; Andrew Jackson's "willingness to put aside immediate gratification and fight for long-term satisfactions" qualified him as Olasky's president-hero. Kati Marton weighed in with *Hidden Power: Presidential Marriages That Shaped Our Recent History,* which claimed that the state of twentieth-century presidential marriages directly affected the fate of the country: "The most confident presidents generally have been the ones with the healthiest respect for their wives." (Perhaps not coincidentally, Marton herself has been the wife of more than one confident national powerhouse: TV anchorman Peter Jennings and former diplomat–U.N. ambassador Richard Holbrooke.) Whether liberal or conservative, historian or journalist, man or woman, *something* about marriage now mattered deeply in American political thinking.

It also becomes clear in retrospect that the much-bemoaned shrinking zone of privacy for politicians was itself only an epiphenomenon of the new spousal politics. As we've seen, a shrinking zone of privacy is companionate coupledom's default mode, known in our time as "intimacy." And electoral politics too was now nothing if not intimate. According to modern relationship credos, partners must know everything there is to know about one another: withholding information or having secrets is a definite warning sign of relationship distress and in principle nothing should be off limits (even if on occasion, "making sure" may be required). If opening a partner's mail or verifying whereabouts also signals relationship distress, well . . . if there's nothing to hide, who needs privacy?

The advent of spousal politics meant that the political realm would now adhere to the same code, demanding from participants the same degree of transparency. Reporters took to picking through candidates' household garbage, and requests for public disclosure of personal information were ratcheted up. Where once financial disclosure forms sufficed, now there were the equivalent of sexual disclosure forms, with reporters playing spousal interrogators, demanding to be told when a candidate had last committed adultery, or substance abuse, or off-color comedy; media klieg lights illuminating every bodily crevice, intimate desire, or embarrassing foible. Recall that this was also the period in which releasing detailed medical records of candidates and presidents became routine, with every condition from seasonal allergies to herpes outbreaks to colonoscopy reports entered into the public record. We could now truly say we knew our representatives inside and out. Even the political spin had that familiar air of marital dissembling, as when the physician of herpes sufferer, senator and presidential candidate John McCain, gamely tried to reassure a nation of sexually suspicious voters that McCain *could* have picked up the virus while a POW in Vietnam, lest anyone infer that he'd contracted it while engaged in a less patriotic activity.

In the new spousal politics—not unrelated to its partner-in-zeitgeist, twelve-step culture—the personal reigned. Testimony and confession were ascendant modes; thinking was subordinated to feeling; ideology mattered less than "character." No longer roped to traditional uptight rationalist forms of oratory like debate, the spouse-politician was no longer even bound by the conventions of "speech" per se. Perhaps "acting out" would be a more accurate description of the millennial rhetorical style: improvised spectacles of yearning and troubling desires and catch-me-if-you-can parlor games performed by the nation's conflicted politician-thespians for an audience of emotionally codependent constituents, our attention glued to their every prevarication. Acting out is hardly unfamiliar territory, doubtless many of us have employed similar rhetorical modes in our own domestic lives or are familiar with its conventions courtesy of our own spouses, if innocent ourselves. But of course acting out *is* the time-honored outlet for conflicts and ambivalences or for those matters about which ordinary language proves too threatening or self-knowledge too scanty. Out of necessity, we spouses become adept at decoding the behavior of our mates, thus allowing things to be "said" without being exactly said, and with the advent of spousal politics, at least we got some additional mileage out of these hard-won skills.

If the '90s was an adulterous decade, it follows that it was a particularly scandalous one too (or how would we know about the adultery?) One of scandal's useful functions is allowing certain kinds of discussions to take place publicly that otherwise wouldn't, providing a social framework for questions about ethics and values to be debated and rehashed. Still, this doesn't in itself account for the particular preoccupation with adultery at this moment: were there no other stories to tell? No other ethical breaches?* Perhaps psychoanalyst Adam Phillips suggests a way of accounting for the fascination with the subject when he remarks that adultery is, at heart, a drama about change. It's a way of trying to invent a world, as he puts it, a way of knowing something about what we may want—and thus, by definition, a political form. After all, articulating visions of change *is* at least part of the job description of those who enter politics—though given the terminal stagnation afflicting the politician imagination in our time, given the chronic long-term failure to produce new political ideas, it's something anyone may be pardoned for forgetting. But if acting out is the spousal communication of choice when explicitness is deemed too radical or desires too inchoate, were we constituents ourselves remiss as well? Might we have been more attentive to what our politician-spouses were trying to express? More supportive? Better help-mates? (How many long-term marriages have foundered at exactly this juncture, when one spouse misses hearing what the other doesn't have the courage to say: *I'm unhappy. I'm bored. I've met someone else.*)

Could there have been a leader more adept at the spousal style than Bill Clinton? If the armchair diagnosis on Clinton was that he "couldn't keep it zipped," clearly there was a

---

*Recall that the Clinton imbroglio began as an inquiry into financial improprieties, which not only failed to seize the public interest, but also that of the special prosecutor assigned to investigate them, who quickly turned his attention to the presidential sex life.

growing collective exhaustion with that enterprise generally. Keeping things zipped was now regarded as emotionally dangerous, or at best, useless: as every therapy habitué
knows, "it" inevitably pops up elsewhere in coded or symptomatic forms, or migrates into addictive and compulsive
behaviors (the decade's most beloved versions of symptomatic behavior). Whatever remnants of 1950s reticence or
the Anglo-American stiff upper lip remained vestigial in
American political culture, the ascendancy of a twelve-step
society and talk show therapeutics as a national emotional
style knocked them from their perch. Prescriptive regimens
of confession and catharsis now dominated political rhetoric; there was an increasing reliance on sentiment as an
index of political credibility. Bill Clinton was much mocked
for once using the phrase "I feel your pain," but it also
set the standard for political speech: all politicians were
now required to show emotion and tell us who they were
"inside." Recall that in 1972 when presidential candidate
Edwin Muskie cried in front of reporters his campaign col-
lapsed as a result; in 2001 when California representative
Gary Condit didn't cry in front of reporters while discussing
the mysterious disappearance of his intern-girlfriend, he
was widely regarded as an unfeeling monster.*

Having feelings was a new entitlement program; express-

---

*Or a murderer. Because indications were that the two had been sexually
involved and Condit refused to admit it in so many words ("I haven't
been a perfect man" was all he would say—his judgment about how to
handle the media proved disastrous at every turn), a level of suspicion
dominated the public discussion and media coverage, often implying that
he was thus capable of anything and probably had a hand in her disappearance. When Condit rather unwisely ran for reelection, hecklers

ing them, a substitute for a national health care policy. But storm clouds were gathering over this weepy scene. The problem occurred when the issue of desire entered the picture, specifically, non-marital desire. It was here that the regime of feelings and the demand for transparency would come head to head, smashed to smithereens on the rocky cliffs of reputation and hypocrisy. The problem, in brief, was this: according to the tenets of popular psychology, feelings must be *expressed,* yet according to tenets of popular morality, non-sanctioned desires must be *repressed.* Our representatives proved as maladroit at negotiating these contradictions as the bridegroom caught sleeping with the maid of honor the night before the wedding: it's really hard not to read it as a sign that something's wrong, no matter how much you have invested in not recognizing there's a problem.

All that was wrong was *fidelity.* Politician marital fidelity had somehow become elevated into something beyond a political requirement: it had begun to resemble a utopian imaginary, or as close to one as the nation seemed capable—as if once transparency between our politicians' private and public lives was achieved, faith in our national institutions could be restored once again. But clearly fidelity

---

shouted, "Where did you bury the body?" Was the path from adulterer to murderer really so direct in the public imagination, or was there something so symbolically laden about adultery during this period that it could stand in for any crime, no matter how heinous or how little actual evidence supported it? The intern's body turned up a year later in a deserted area of a D.C. park; it appeared that she'd been attacked while jogging. No evidence ever connected Condit to the disappearance; he remained a figure of national opprobrium and shunning nevertheless.

also couldn't bear up to the scrutiny it had courted. However much doggedly upholding outdated vows was touted as the only virtue worth having, here were our own representatives doing the wild thing, swinging to a whole different beat. What was a poor constituent to think? Maybe that dogged fidelity really isn't all it's touted to be? That outdated vows should be rewritten, not just blindly reaffirmed? After all, restlessness and dissatisfaction have also had a certain cachet in America's story about itself: was that frontier mythos bubbling to the surface once again too? It was all very confusing, and by millennium's end, the whole moral-political consensus was starting to look a little tattered around the edges.

The vow is a crossover language, performed when assuming political office or taking a spouse. In fact, marriage has long provided a metaphor for fidelity to the nation, historian Nancy Cott points out, with the marriage bond providing a convenient symbol for the social contract that produces a government. Households aren't just training grounds for citizenship and allegiance to contracts, they're small governments in themselves, and like the democratic nation, they must be founded on the illusion of loving partnership. Both marriages and governments represent supposedly freely chosen structures of authority and obligation. Like companionate marriages, democracies too are supposed to rule through consent, not coercion, meaning that the appearance of free choice should never be called into question. (Which isn't to say that democracies won't quickly act to protect their legitimacy if challenged, relying on everything from covert surveillance to armed force, even when the challenge comes from their own citizenry.) But from the state's point of view, marriage isn't only a good metaphor, it's a public value in its own right, a far better system for maintaining social order than a land of free-floating, unmoored desires. As a bonus it facilitates governmental sorties into citizen's private lives: note that the introduction of marriage licenses was just one of the various new forms of population management that modern statehood ushered into being, from numbering citizens to mandatory education. (Historical footnote: marriages were once private agreements between individuals, usually undertaken as property arrangements. First the church stepped in to claim authority over them, and then the state, in both cases consolidating their own fledgling institutional power by exerting control over what had once been common-law practices.)

Why should the state license marriages, by the way? Don't ask, just play along because if you do, the state will show its gratitude by conferring numerous special privileges on you: there are reportedly over a thousand places in federal law where marriage confers benefits not allotted to the nonmarried. (And arguably why the fight for gay marriage takes up the wrong battle: rather than marriage as a prerequisite to access government privileges, shouldn't the fight be to uncouple resource distribution from marital status?) In exchange for its munificence, the state asks just a teensy courtesy from you in return: fidelity to its particular vision of marriage. This would be the Christian ideal of lifelong monogamy: one wife per husband, one sex partner each, for eternity. (This makes adultery not only an infidelity to your spouse but also to your country, and it is still illegal in more than a few particularly jittery locales. As of 1988, forty-five states still had some form of adultery laws on the books.) If you prefer to think the state's vision of love and yours are in such happy coincidence that there's no point in worrying about it, let's remember that the state's vision long required racial purity as well—miscegenation laws were still in force in a number of states until overruled by the Supreme Court in 1967.

Despite the official line that the United States has no state religion, the Christian model of marriage is lodged so deeply within American political theory and statehood that they're effectively interdependent. This makes the matter of polygamy—illegal in every state—an interesting problem. Outlawing it was made a condition of Utah's attaining statehood and a federal act was created to ban it; when the occasional noncompliant Mormon surfaces in the Utah hinterlands these days, it's more than a local scandal: it's a national affront. Regardless of whether the marriages are consensual—or as consensual as any marriage entered into under religious and familial pressures—the premise appears to be that consenting to monogamy must be consensual, but consenting to polygamy can only be coercion. Thus the women involved (even those proclaiming consent) are damsels wronged who need state protection from illicit male desires—and from their own—which affords brain-jarring opportunities to hear female protectionism in the guise of women's-rights rhetoric emerge from the mouths of lawmakers typically indifferent to feminism in every other instance. Here, for instance, is Utah senator Ron Allen, defending a state polygamy prosecution: "We are giving women and children an opportunity to set their own direction and have a sense of freedom in their lives."* (What Allen does not say is that in order to achieve this goal, state officials are breaking up families against the participants' own wishes in order to create single-mother households—which state officials are also supposed to be against.) Here is Senator Allen's rather tortured rationale for prosecution:

> It's come to my attention in the past couple of years that there are a number of human rights violations in our state in these closed societies. Some are the same types of crimes that occur in non-polygamous society, such as child abuse and incest, but also welfare and tax fraud. There is a preponderance of empirical evidence that these crimes are quite common and may even have the tacit approval of some community members.

One wants to point out to Senator Allen that if these are "closed societies," it's precisely because they're illegal. One might also like to ask him whether welfare and tax fraud actually qualify as human rights abuses. But you almost feel sorry for a politician trying to produce a coherent explana-

---

*In this case a polygamist named Tom Green was tried and convicted despite the fact that only one of his five marriages was state licensed. Prosecutors successfully argued that even though these were private consensual arrangements they were still felonious, since monogamy is "public policy." Green faced up to twenty-five years in prison and $25,000 in fines; he was eventually sentenced to five years and agreed to reimburse the state $20,000 in benefits paid out to his wives and twenty-nine children. Utah officials estimate that there are as many as fifty thousand citizens living in plural marriages, and openly acknowledged that Green was singled out for prosecution because he kept going on TV to proselytize about it.

tion about a completely incoherent issue. The problems suffered by plural families, as Allen acknowledges in spite of himself, are exactly the same problems afflicting all families to the extent that they're "closed," which—as feminists have long charged—does indeed provide a sanctuary for the abuse of women and children. Patterns of family pathology clearly don't change with the number of wives on the premises.

As we see, it's also impossible to say exactly why polygamy is illegal. (Because it makes the Christian guys too envious?) The reason is that it's against the law—in fact a third-degree felony. But how was it that the state obtained the right to say which marriages can be performed or dissolved and on what basis? Recall that until recently, divorces could be legally obtained only on limited grounds like desertion, adultery, or physical violence, which made marriage the one form of contract where the parties involved couldn't release themselves by mutual agreement. The state had to agree too, as if it were an injured lover refusing to let go once things were over.

But despite the tendency to treat the American-style nuclear family as derived from nature and alternative practices as threatening social pathologies, the sheer number of laws required to enforce monogamous heterosexual marriages in itself contradicts the claim: clearly the conditions of marriage are created and upheld entirely through the multiplicity of laws and norms that happen to be in operation, whatever they are. Consider polyandry (multiple husbands!) should this one day become a feminist demand. With a package of tax incentives attached, wouldn't it soon seem like the most natural thing in the world?

Revamped divorce laws make it clear that social institutions can develop elasticity when threatened with their own demise; when too much rebellion stirs the ranks. Such shifts are often counted (at least by some) as social progress: interracial coupling ceased to be illegal; contraception laws were overturned; marital rape was outlawed; men started sharing the housework. (Some men.) The Christian ideal of lifelong monogamy yielded to serial monogamy, and even elected officials may now practice it within limits—though any politician with more than one divorce under his or her belt will likely find fundraising tough going. But one man's social progress is another's social decay: the conservative response has been to lobby to make divorce more difficult to obtain and to promote so-called covenant marriages—currently an option in three southern states—which makes incompatibility insufficient grounds for divorce and requires lengthy waiting periods to dissolve a marriage. But ironically, despite the conservative premise that more religion would solve all America's problems, it turns out that religion is actually bad for marriage. Figures from the 1998 census indicated that divorce rates in Bible Belt states were roughly 50 percent above the national average, and that rates are actually lowest in more secular states like New York. Responding to what he described as "a marital emergency," one Bible Belt governor proposed to divert federal welfare funds from benefits into campaigns to reduce divorce rates. (Who needs food stamps: you can have intact marriages instead of dinner.) Another Bible Belt governor chose to turn the blame on his own state's ministers. "These divorce statistics are a scalding indictment of what isn't being said behind the pulpit," he charged; under attack, the poor ministers began refusing to marry couples who hadn't had "premarital counseling."

What did this counseling consist of? Parishioners were instructed to "expect less from marriage."

Right around the same time, a Wright State University professor from the burgeoning field of academic marriage research made headlines with the same conclusion. A survey of 522 couples found that many marriages started off with high levels of quality and then declined. If couples would just prepare themselves for these declines, the professor announced, things would be fine. The homily of the moment, from pulpits both holy and academic, was that lowered expectations would solve all our private dilemmas—and incidentally it came just as lowered expectations were being thrust down the nation's throats on the economic front, in a decade of corporate downsizing and layoffs, of slashes in social programs and benefits, and of widening inequality. Just as our Bible Belt ministers were preaching lowered expectations, our Congressional Budget Office was releasing figures showing that the income disparity between rich and poor had doubled since 1977, with the top 1 percent of the country earning as much as the bottom 100 million in after-tax dollars—a gap that had grown so much that four out of five households were earning less as a percentage of the total economic pie than in 1977, despite working longer hours, and slashing vacation time. Median income did rise during this period, but only because families were working longer hours. In fact they were working harder for the same pay: wages were stagnant. (And once recession hit a few years later, the extra work quickly disappeared.)

Was there protest in the streets? No, not quite, but perhaps the protest took a more subtle form, as across the nation an obstinate citizenry began refusing to accept lowered expectations as a norm—in their marriages, that is. The Ask Less from Life plan as the basis for long-term coupledom was failing to secure adherents, and even this tiny protest was being regarded by officialdom, local and federal, as a national emergency, as if it harbored negative implications for national stability. And perhaps it does. After all, if both marriage and citizenship are vow-making enterprises—indeed romantic enterprises—divorce is what severs those vows; if marriages are dissolvable—and at the partner's own behest—then what of the union? If contracts and commitments can be overturned merely on grounds of dissatisfaction, or not getting what you think you should, then what of governments? What happens when the romance fades and you start to see things more clearly?

This is not just a recent national dilemma, it's a longstanding problem. If marriages can't be dissolved, how can the illusion of consensual democracy be maintained? As Nancy Cott points out, that would be sovereignty, not democracy. But if they *are* dissolvable, everything they symbolize is up for grabs too. We do live in a nation founded on a Declaration of Independence, after all—indeed, on a collective divorce, our rather stormy one from Britain. Independence versus fidelity, pursuing happiness versus deferring to established regimes and institutions: such are the split identifications embedded in our already bifurcated national self-understanding—and in our nation's own history, and so many of our popular cultural forms, from road movies to domestic sitcoms—even in our mottos: *Semper fidelis.* The analogies between divorce and revolution hover just below consciousness; so apparently does the anxiety the subject provokes. Meaning don't think about issuing any independence declarations these days or throwing any Boston Tea Parties of your own, because you'll have the FBI on your doorstep in record time.

Which brings us back to our present dilemma. In one corner, serial monogamy: dissolving one couple to embark on another, typically in short order, and with the same high hopes. It's clear that serial monogamy evolved as a pressure-release valve to protect the system from imploding. No, there's nothing wrong with the institution or its premises, no, *you* just happened to get the wrong person. But next time around you'd better make the best of it, because too many strikes and you're out—you're the problem. In serial monogamy, the players change but the institution remains the same: liberal reformism writ familial. In the other corner, adultery: mocking the conventions, throwing cherry bombs at the institution; small-scale social sabotage, the anarcho-syndicalism of private life. No, it's not hard to see why the concept itself might pose a threat to the national project, among other illusory stabilities—these being unstable conventions that hope to appear eternal, typically rummaging through the aesthetic conventions of classicism to buttress themselves: picture government buildings, inaugurals, weddings costumes. But rest assured that adultery doesn't entirely want to smash the system either: where would adultery be without marriage—it requires it!

All things considered, it's still curious that adultery's most public practitioners in millennial America would have been the very cadre whose lives and careers are dedicated to *serving* the union and *representing* its interest; that it would be those high-flying functionaries and elected officials most deeply identified with upholding social conventions—and more importantly, the appearance of conventionality—who would so flagrantly court exposure as mutineers and seditionists. Of course the citizenship-as-marriage analogy has proven remarkably elastic, flexible enough to be reconfigured entirely differently and for opposing purposes over the span of a couple of centuries. In recent memory we've seen it played out by every different side: it hasn't been only conservatives who've been gripped by the issue. Recall that '60s-era activists also propelled conjugal issues onto the national agenda, diagnosing the mores of the bourgeois couple and American-style sexual repression (or "phallic masculinity," in the feminist version of the argument) as domestic analogues of U.S. warfare in Vietnam—the missionary position on an international scale; our national pathology. Popular culture took up the diagnosis too, as in the 1978 antiwar movie *Coming Home:* set at the height of the Vietnam era, a dutiful uptight housewife suffers through terrible sex with her military officer husband, then has her first orgasm with a paraplegic vet–war protester and becomes politicized herself.*

But well before the 1960s—over a century before—ques-

---

*Any historically retrospective film—as *Coming Home* was—always has a presentist agenda too: here we can watch a '70s-era reconfiguration of masculinity in the making. Real men don't go off and fight wars, they stay home and perform oral sex on their women. Masculinity measured in female orgasms rather than the foreign body count or other achievements in male-only arenas was a new cinematic masculine ideal: only ten years earlier, cinemagoers were watching John Wayne win the Vietnam war in *The Green Berets,* clearly battling not just the Viet Cong, but the girly pacifists at home.

tions of love, marriage, divorce, fidelity, and sexual freedom were consistently linked to civic ideals in political debates. According to historian John Spurlock, the marriage-citizenship parallel was intrinsic to the tenor of mid-nineteenth-century political discourse. Then, as now, the fate of marriage was linked to the fate of the nation; unhappy marriages were suspected of undermining the national social fabric. If marriage was the primary social contract, then inauthenticity in marriage endangered the legitimacy of other social bonds; if marital regimentation deadened feeling, what were the possibilities of a flourishing, inventive nation?

Apparently even a hundred and fifty years ago, marriage was perceived as an inherently shaky institution, and the same inadequate remedies abounded. As in our day, marital advice manuals were a flourishing industry; however, unlike now, alongside them were journals and books devoted to exploring the possibilities of conjugal reform, even to critiquing the institution itself. Demands to abolish marriage and institute free love were reigning topics of public debate, promoted by assorted freethinkers, socialists, and transcendentalists (the philosophy associated with Emerson), or under the rubric of foreign imports like Owenism, Fourierism, or within homegrown social movements that Spurlock terms "middle-class radicalism." These were mainstream discussions, not fringe movements: town meetings on alternate forms of marriage were a frequent feature of antebellum America and the most contrarian ideas were seriously entertained. Perhaps not everyone is formed for constancy in love? Or as marriage reformer Paul Brown put it in the 1830s, scoffing at the idea that anyone could genuinely guarantee marital fidelity for life: "Now if any person were to make so rash a bargain about any other sort of transaction, our laws would rate him *non compos mentis* and from thence make the obligation void." Or this from the influential nineteenth-century British radical William Godwin, later to marry early feminist Mary Wollstonecraft, the author of *Vindication of the Rights of Woman:* "It is absurd to expect the inclinations and wishes of two human beings to coincide, through any long period of time. To oblige them to act and live together is to subject them to some inevitable portion of thwarting, bickering, and unhappiness."

Social reform and renewal were still viewed as actual possibilities; a spirit of experimentalism was in the air. Questioning social institutions was a permissible activity, even if no reassuring answers were forthcoming: Why not at least entertain the possibility that there could be forms of daily life based on something other than isolated households and sexually exclusive couples? Why not confront rather than ignore the reality of disappointment and the deadening routinization that pervades married households? Maybe confronting the flaws in married life would be a route to reforming a flawed society? Maybe reforming the fabric of individual relationships was the path toward political renewal? Social institutions should exist to "perfect and ennoble individual man," or as reformer Henry C. Wright put it in 1855:

Society is full of inharmonious and most fatal alliances between men and women, under the name of marriage,— alliances as unnatural and monstrous, and as fruitful of evil, as a union between liberty and slavery, truth and falsehood, purity and impurity,—alliances in which no compromises can ever produce harmony or happiness.

Such social critiques weren't confined to town halls alone, they were also tested out in a network of utopian communities operating across the country and which flourished for various lengths of time despite endemic economic obstacles. The best known were Brook Farm in Massachusetts, New Harmony in Indiana, and Oneida in upstate New York, but similar communities, often with a few thousand members, sprung up in Ohio, Pennsylvania, and farther west. Typically they allied themselves with the other progressive issues of the day—antislavery activism and women's rights, educational reform, alternative child-rearing models—guided by various philosophical principles about free love, social reformism, and equity between the sexes. Maybe it was the openness of a still relatively young nation, Spurlock suggests, that allowed for a spirit of greater possibility and allowed ordinary people to think that they could reinvent their lives if they chose—and that doing so might even affect the political direction of the country. Today this is rather an unthinkable premise: consider the obligatory mockery of the 1960s, whose sartorial experiments have so conveniently allowed the entire notion of a counterculture to fade into history as naïve and silly, as if all social protest were the political counterpart of paisley and love beads, as if transforming the country—or anything—was a wacky idea. Other than transforming your own abs of course, which *is* taken very seriously. Self-improvement reigns, having absorbed all the transformative energies once directed at the social, or at anything beyond an individual stomach.

Reassembling these shards of buried national history offers one way of thinking about how adultery might come to play a starring role in subsequent civic life as the country's most ambivalent political metaphor. If marriage did once figure in national debates as an analogy for social stagnation, if marital experimentation is lodged in our nation's history as a paradigm for political experimentation, if "looking elsewhere" is invariably a response to dissatisfaction, then what will future historians make of our own recent contribution to the story: so many prominent national personages parading their unfulfilled desires before the electorate, restaging this conflicted national story in furtive experimental communities of two? Adultery may be rather a downscaled rendering of those heroic experimental communities past, but we do inhabit a social climate of privatization and lowered expectations these days, after all.

If experimentalism was once publicly possible and openly debated, if now such discussions are played out surreptitiously and behind closed doors, exposed to view only courtesy of scandal, does this make scandal a media society's substitute for the town forum? Like town forums, scandals provide venues for staging social issues, for negotiating social boundaries and possibilities, for having ethical debates— unlike town forums, the opportunity for sustained reflection is not incredibly high. Outrage substitutes for thought and vicariousness for social criticism, exposé for principled discussion. None of this makes scandal a demonstration of enlightened or progressive thinking, and politically speaking the outcomes are unpredictable. Sometimes boundaries are expanded—consider the numerous behaviors once regarded as scandalous which now aren't, like out-of-wedlock births. In other cases, boundaries are reestablished and transgressors exiled—founding cultural taboos like murder and incest obviously don't shift categories.* And so what of adultery, scandalizing a nation for more than a decade, riding into town on the heels of exposé, demanding everyone's attention: the issue of the decade, or so said the news magazines. What made it so worth paying attention to: in other words, what makes a scandal scandalous at one moment and a yawn the next?

Literary critics tell us that in genres devoted to exposing secrets, protagonists and spectators propel these plots forward because something previously hidden needs knowing. As the spate of national adultery scandals unfolded over the course of a decade, it did start to feel rather literary and familiar, like an update on Poe's *Purloined Letter*, with the incriminating evidence carefully hidden in full view. The plot seemed recycled, verging on farce: faithless marital citizens cast as the dastardly criminal class, cooperatively playing along by scattering incriminating clues for a delighted nation of amateur gumshoes. "Prove it," challenged presidential candidate Gary Hart during the 1988 campaign, when the media—in a preview of the adulterous decade to come—suspected him of cheating on his wife. True to form, he turned out to be hiding the perfectly cast Donna Rice in

---

*Though ways of accounting for them might, as we've seen with the newfound popularity of trauma and family repetition in the vocabulary of behavior and motive.

plain sight—or in this case, on the deck of a yacht called *Monkey Business* cruising toward Bimini; shortly thereafter, photos of the nautically garbed blonde model perched on Hart's lap hit the front pages. (It didn't require Poe's mastermind-of-detection Dupin to solve that one.)

Detective stories, like scandal stories, do have an addictive quality, even when the solution is clear from miles away. The advantage of fiction is that you find out who's to blame in the end; unfortunately, things aren't often quite so clear-cut in life. Adam Phillips says that suspicion is, at root, a philosophy of hope; jealousy is secretly a form of optimism: "It makes us believe that there is something to know and something worth knowing." But as you're rifling your mate's handbag or wallet, or scouring the tabloids, consider: whether it's spouses or politicians or celebrities under scrutiny, isn't that "something" also already known? Outing politicians as adulterers is an epistemological exercise about as useful as rediscovering the laws of gravity: if you sit under an apple tree long enough, sooner or later a piece of ripe fruit will hit you on the head, but what's the point? It would only be useful if the laws of gravity were subject to recurring bouts of amnesia and were thus a perpetual surprise.

If detection plots, snooping, and scandal are ways of acquiring knowledge, they also always involve more than the particulars of any one crime. After all, crime and social transgression—including adultery—have meaning only in relation to the rules of a social order, which makes these deeply cultural stories, not individual ones alone. (Exposing hidden truths inevitably involves founding social taboos: any mystery that needs solving exposes something about society as a whole.) But there's also a rather distressing double bind inherent in the snooping enterprise. Do you really want your suspicions confirmed? As the cuckolded say on the soaps, *"I want some answers!"* But . . . really? Consider the consequences: destabilizing changes, uncertain futures, putting things up for grabs—or the two scariest words in the English language: *property settlement.*

Fidelity pledges, whether to nations or marriages, do hold particular property relations in place: break those vows and anything might happen. Sentimentality should not cause us to lose sight of the fact that marriage always was and is an economic institution; additionally, that private property always required monogamous marriage to insure patrilineal property distribution through inheritance. (A distribution that is only really ensured to the extent that wives can be convinced to bed only their own husbands, one explanation for why women's sexuality was always more closely policed than men's. And why women need to be inculcated with a higher degree of sexual repression than men, so that bedding anyone but their own husbands would be all the more unthinkable.) If this mattered more in an era when wealth was based on landholdings rather than on more recent forms of cultural capital like professional expertise, the old ideology and its moral codes still linger—finding other rationales and justifications to attach themselves to as necessary. Now monogamy is required for general stability and "the national fabric" rather than the transmission of family estates: same medicine, new package.

Let's not forget that nations too organize property relations, and citizenship signifies our fidelity to them. (Or supposedly does: when did we make this pledge exactly?)

That the whole business of political consent is itself rather *fictive* may account for why love needs to be configured as a backup system, an auxiliary political institution. Any nation's property laws exist to protect whatever class holds state power—even when that class is the state, as we saw in the yonder days of state socialism. But, after all, where would our own wealthy elites be—corporate or private—without the last-instance threat of standing armies to back up the rule of property law, just in case anyone gets any funny ideas about redistributing things? In short, what an accumulation of history and economics, bloodshed and coercion, can be packed into that funny sentimental little word "fidelity"; and what a morass of tangled anxious ideas about it resides deep down in the national unconscious.

Allegories and myths are ways that societies keep track of their contradictions; new ones are constructed as required. Given this new insecurity on the part of the electorate about the fidelity of our representatives, was there some new anxiety about the fidelity of the institutions of representation themselves, in the waning years of the twentieth century? Was the Union itself in trouble? If the much-noted national consensus-shift from JFK-era adultery license to Clinton-era adultery culpability implies that a national allegory was being rewritten (and inscribed on the leader's body, as in all mythologies worth their admission price), the update casts the citizenry in the role of insecure wife, continually suspecting and fearing perfidy. With the national press increasingly devoted to nosing out adultery scandals, and the tabloids paying off mistresses for their stories before the sheets were even dry, with television interviewers playing couples therapists in tearful primetime confessionals, electoral politics was being reconfigured as a stagnant marriage, and didn't we, the wives, waiting at home, secretly know it? Look at the apathy of the last few elections: we were just going through the motions. The romance died long ago. We're being cheated and duped: his promises are lies, his vows a joke. We're a nation of cuckolds, who *know* we're being strung along and played for fools. But lacking dignity, schooled—as wives so often are—in passivity and pragmatism, armed with our subtle little payback techniques, we can just lie back and think of a balanced budget, or assuage our resentment with over-consumption, from junk food to junk culture, like bored suburban housewives all. (Any gender can play.)

Feeling vulnerable? Anxious? Ignored? Suspect somewhere in your heart of hearts that things are going sour? Or—as any marriage counselor will inquire at the first tearful session—is there something that you just aren't getting from this union of yours that you would need to feel secure in its embrace?

Well, who wouldn't be feeling taken advantage of? Given the economic restructuring underway in late capitalism's transnationalist incarnation, with the Western economies becoming increasingly tightfisted, refusing to live up to their most basic vows, systematically dismantling the welfare state, unwilling to provide even the most minimal economic safety nets—even decent health care is now asking too much!—these days anyone can be cavalierly abandoned with barely a few week's notice, like so many discarded middle-aged wives, traded in for younger, cheaper, foreign, or more technologically adept models. Feeling unloved? Join the club—the New Economy, that is. Actually, you've been automatically enrolled. Now try getting out.

Allegories may be ways of telling collective narratives, but let's not forget, these are individual stories too. Note that in the vast barrage of media attention to adultery, in the microscopic scrutiny of every blemish and "distinguishing mark" on the politician body, the question of just what these adulterer-representatives of ours were *seeking* in those nondomestic beds and yachts and hotel rooms was simply never asked.* *What* could be so compelling that risking everything for a few moments in the semipublic arms of interns, groupies, congressional pages, or hookers seems like a risk worth taking? Simply sex? (Is sex ever simply sex?) How exactly did this pride of hardened political animals, careers laboriously constructed move by move over lifetimes of canniness and mistrust, come to display such alarmingly faulty judgment, along with all their vulnerabilities and desires, so unabashedly—so very *nakedly*—before the prying eyes of fellow citizens and hanging judges? What form of unconsciousness was this at work?

Cynics and a certain variety of feminist will tell us the answer is simply power: either the desire for more or the expectation of its limitless protection. But thanks to the tabloidization of political life, we social detectives became the recipients of numerous blow-by-blow accounts of the

---

*Bill Clinton's sexual harassment accuser Paula Jones said she could prove that Clinton had exposed himself to her because she could identify "distinguishing marks" on his penis. A joke going around at the time was that the "distinguishing mark" must have been a map of Bosnia.

pillow talk of the powerful, each one making it more clear than the last that these affairs are conducted not under the sign of power, but that of pathos.

Exhibit A: The Clinton–Lewinsky affair, which, thanks to the special prosecutor's 445-page report (and 3,000-page appendix) and Lewinsky's subsequent biography and television interviews, was the most thoroughly documented such episode in history. Sure, there was sex—of sorts—but more than that, there were the shared stories about fat childhoods, the dumb little presents, the lonely late-night phone calls. The only thing that was shocking about any of this— at least, in our former president's case—was risking so much for so little, as if the supplement were actually far more imperative than the thing being supplemented.

And wasn't this what enraged the country; wasn't this Bill Clinton's crime? It's not precisely adultery that's prohibited (after all, politicians have been doing it for centuries and everyone knows it), it's public acknowledgment that the system needs propping up with these secret forms of enjoyment. The Starr Report kindly included Monica's recollection of Clinton's remark that he hadn't had oral sex in a long time. What exactly does "breaking vows" mean here except not accommodating to the not-enoughness of what's supposed to suffice, and in such a flamboyant and public way that there was no mistaking it? Let's recall that the marriage vow isn't only to a spouse, it's to the institution and to every strained metaphor that it sustains, and to every other relationship and household and ego defense sustained by it in turn. Clearly if there were a Starr Report on every American marriage, the institution would instantly crumble, never to recover. And what, then, of the republic? Citizens obviously have a duty to lie about their sex lives, as Clinton himself knew—and tried valiantly to do. (Then again, there's knowing and there's knowing, as Clinton also so perfectly exemplified.)

Exhibit B: A few years before the Lewinsky story broke, Clintonian homunculus Dick Morris managed to get himself into a similar flap, like a test balloon for the main show to come. If history always repeats itself, this time it was farce the first time around too. Morris, a charmless, pugnacious, unscrupulous (even by Washington standards) top political advisor to Clinton, credited with moving Clinton rightward and stealing the family values rhetoric out from under the Republican platform—also noted for switching political loyalties opportunistically and for doing whatever it took to get his candidate's poll numbers up, whatever sacrifice of principles it required, and thus for his supposedly unparalleled political "shrewdness"—so wanted to impress the prostitute he was involved with that he invited her to eavesdrop on phone conversations he conducted with the president from their hotel suite. What's a national security violation or two between intimates? He was also reportedly prone to pillow talk about classified matters such as the covert presence of U.S. warships in Cuban waters, since as every aspiring Don Juan knows, nothing turns a woman on more than hemispheric military prowess. (Guys: running low on baseball stats at a crucial moment? Try the Monroe Doctrine.)

In this case, unfortunately, the affection was one-way and leaned heavily on shopworn myths about heart-of-gold hookers who, unlike Morris, don't sell their loyalties to the highest bidder. Apparently never having seen *Pretty Woman*, failing to have taken the important lessons of *Irma La*

Douce sufficiently to heart, his paramour turned out to be surreptitiously recording their romps together for sale to the *Star,* a national tabloid, even luring Morris onto their terrace, hotel bathrobe flapping in the breeze, so photographers stationed across the way could snap a few compromising photos. Maybe it was rather touching that Morris—married, of course—mistook his plush expense-account hotel suite for an enclave governed by sentiment not commerce: the human capacity for optimism is no doubt one of the better things about us as a species. Nevertheless, Morris became the butt of every national joke imaginable and predictably was forced to resign when his confidante proceeded to reveal not just the details of his mildly kinky sexual preferences (something to do with toes), but far worse for him, the extent of his naïvely misplaced trust.

What went virtually unnoticed in all the subsequent moral hullabaloo (over the Morris incident, but also about every other D.C. sex scandal of the decade) was the simple fact that toxic levels of everyday dissatisfaction, boredom, unhappiness, and not-enoughness are the functional norms in millions of lives and marriages. Hidden in plain sight, as it were: because this is the condition that so many of us know, tacitly agree to, and, to various degrees of severity, rue. This is the price of stability, or so we're assured. The unforgivable social crime is calling attention to its not-enoughness by getting yourself exposed trying to remedy it.

Yet also note that an entire scandal industry exists to expose *what everyone already knows.* Knowing, not knowing; exposing, forgetting. Beware the scandal machinery busy at work trying to catch you in the act of assuaging boredom, or capturing a few moments of happiness, and the higher placed on the national social ladder you are—that is, the more emblematic you are (ordinary individuals generally fail to be emblematic)—the more careful you're advised to be. Just another of those interesting national "contradictions" that make America what it is today.

A question to the nation: *Is* boredom socially necessary? There's no doubt that it's prevalent. Says Judith Seifer, former president of the American Association of Sex Educators, Counselors, and Therapists: "Sexual boredom is the most pandemic dysfunction in this country." Or as philosopher Denis de Rougemont puts it in *Love in the Western World,* regarding our penchant for fetishizing stability as a facile solution to love's dilemmas: "To wish marriage to be based on such 'happiness' implies in men and women today a capacity for boredom which is almost morbid." (Apparently not one given to optimism on the subject, he also wonders whether there's just something fatal to marriage at the heart of human longing.)

Let us approach the question of boredom from two interconnected angles—love and work—which have, after all, been the recurring themes of our discussion. We'll begin with work.

When the assembly line was introduced to the workforce, and the system that would come to be known as Fordism began to dominate industrial production, it marked something of a turning point in the history of boredom. Was this an inevitable social development? It's true that within three months of the introduction of the endless-chain conveyer in 1914, the time it took to assemble a Model T dropped to one-tenth the time it had previously taken. It's true as well that this new division of labor instantly transformed work into inhumanly boring drudgery, but the presumption was that profit took precedence over trivial considerations like satisfaction in work or the quality of workers' lives. It's also true that these productivity increases could be transformed into bigger profits for owners and shareholders, and that those profits were not passed on to the bored workers themselves—or not directly, since wages were never tied to profit. (Antonio Gramsci, writing about Ford's labor innovations, charged that brutal cynicism was required to institute such a system, and that the human toll was "automatic mechanical attitudes." Mindless mechanical jobs produced a corresponding intellectual life in those doing them, said Gramsci, and if the new system of production required "a new type of man," the ideal type for this system would be a trained gorilla.*)

Henry Ford did however significantly raise wages for his workers, and higher wages meant that the intellectual atrophy and physical injuries resulting from jobs requiring repetitive motion were at least somewhat compensated by the new ability of workers to purchase the cheap commodities spit out at the end of the ever more ubiquitous production lines. We humans do turn out to be infinitely creative at finding ways to replace what's been extracted from our lives— health, creativity, and pride, for example—by other means.

---

*Antonio Gramsci was an Italian political philosopher whose anti-fascist activities unfortunately got him thrown in prison, which was where he spent the last ten tormented years of his life (under Mussolini's personal supervision). His prison writings—notably on how "common sense" is conscripted for political hegemony—were published only posthumously.

As everyone knows (and if not, the advertising industry was invented to educate you on this score), steady doses of the proper commodities *will* help assuage the sense of amputation and resentment that comes from doing a mindlessly boring thing for most of your life on earth—or will as long as you keep up those payments—easy credit being another nifty way of ensuring workers' loyalty to mind-numbing jobs. This is both brilliant and efficient: transforming bored workers into avid consumers perpetuates a healthy production-consumption cycle which, as Gramsci pointed out, also extends beyond an economic system alone: it's an emotional system too. After all, we don't just check our psychologies at the door when we clock in.

Not long before Ford came onto the scene, Marx had coined the term "commodity fetishism," by which he meant— or would have, could he have imagined such wonders—that lavishing love on your stereo system or maintaining an erotic relation to your sportscar is not entirely unrelated to your degree of alienation from your job: a form of compensation for something lost or missing, namely the creativity and satisfaction that can come from meaningful work. Along comes Henry Ford, sufficiently visionary to retail a fundamentally Marxian concept for corporate profit by offering workers high enough wages to promote consumption while cunningly roping them into the emerging production-consumption system—though of course without the profit-sharing that might eventually also offer financial independence from it.

Expecting pleasure or satisfaction from work is now a mark of job privilege: labor economist Michael Zweig estimates that 62 percent of the U.S. labor force—white- and blue-collar both—have no control or authority over the pace or content of their work, which is Zweig's updated definition of "working class." The new economy, or the post-Fordism of our time—capital flight, de-skilling of labor, growth of the service and information sectors—has hardly made work more interesting. The basic premises of the Fordist model are now so deeply knitted into the fabric of social life in our time—boredom as a job requirement, pleasure as supplementary—that you can barely tell them apart.

So the point is this. The necessity for compensatory forms of satisfaction—for *supplements*—was structured into the whole setup from its inception, a setup, as Gramsci tells us, both economic and emotional. Or, to make the argument in reverse, the necessity for supplements is a reliable index of the alienation present in the setup at any moment (a formula that applies whether you're hard at work, or working hard at that relationship), and this is obviously now delinked from any particular occupation or social rank. Even presidents can be afflicted.

Incidentally, Henry Ford raised workers' pay, but only as long as they maintained upstanding domestic lives. Proof of marital status was required to earn the higher wages; so was keeping sexual and drinking proclivities in check. Investigators from Ford's so-called Sociological Department were regularly sent to workers' homes to investigate their domestic situations and report back to headquarters. With Ford an early "family values" booster, the economic undertones of the contemporary message become a little clearer: married workers are productive workers, which means more profits for someone—though not for the workers themselves, still scraping around to assuage their boredom with compensatory forms, from over-consumption to love. (Let's not even get into American fatness!) Love, an infinitely malleable thing, shaping itself to whatever necessity is currently required, fits the bill as well as or better than other available substances; in commodity culture it conforms to the role of a cheap commodity, spit out at the end of the assembly line in cookie-cutter forms, marketed to bored and alienated producer-consumers as an all-purpose salve to emptiness.*

Which brings us back to love. (And emptiness.)

The national media reacted with some amusement when, at decade's end, it was revealed that the ranking Republican state senator from Indiana, one Steven R. Johnson, had engaged in an extramarital affair with a twenty-three-year-old college intern employed in his office. It was the Clinton-Lewinsky imbroglio writ small, and hence the mirth—amidst pro forma demands for "an investigation" and calls for the senator's resignation. In this case however, unlike our dissembling president, state senator Johnson simply confessed and expressed regret. He refused the calls to resign. He accepted the results of a voice vote removing him from his committee chairmanships, and banishing him to a seat in the back of the chamber for two years. (Given the zeal for humiliation on the part of his colleagues, one begins to

---

*It must be added that in raising questions about the compensatory aspects of commodity culture we must also be careful to avoid the annoying moralizing asceticism and false rectitude sometimes associated with this line of thinking. The anti-wrinkle cycle on my automatic dryer *is* an authentic pleasure, and shoe shopping *is* clearly preferable as a leisure activity to gathering around a campfire playing homemade musical instruments and singing labor anthems.

wonder what percentage of those voting for banishment did so under temporary amnesia about their own dalliances.) Senator Johnson, however, whose marriage ended as a result of the affair, took a more philosophical view of these procedures, praising his colleagues for their "civility and grace" and announcing in a public statement that "in a very strange sense" he had been given "a fascinating opportunity to start life anew."

It would be interesting to know what exactly Johnson's colleagues wanted to investigate. As with our snooping spouses, what answers weren't already known? Did they wish to investigate Johnson's rather surprising endorsement of fascination and renewal? His apparent pleasure at finding himself in a different position than the one he'd become accustomed to? True, touting transformation and risk-taking *is* a rather novel political vision, especially coming from a politician. What lobbyists are pushing it? What PACs are financing it? But with so much yearning and dissatisfaction so pervasive and so constitutive that they're hidden in plain sight, at the epicenter of national political life, it becomes hard to refute the idea that *something's* missing, something that adultery in its fumbling way attempts to palliate, under conditions of enforced secrecy, thus dictating behavior ranging from ludicrous and risky to deeply unconscious. Rather hard to refute the thought that a simple ineradicable desire for *more* motored a decade-plus of national scandal.

The only secret left to expose was that even our *politicians* are such clandestine utopians, so burdened with excess desires and imagination and yearnings that despite lifetimes of hard-nosed pragmatism and years of schooling in realpolitik, renunciation doesn't work, even for them. And so it emerged, if in a backhanded fashion, that America *is* a functioning representational democracy after all: the current version just works in reverse, with our politicians representing to us constituents back home the impossibility of living by the norms of conventional domestic intimacy that they spouted out the other sides of their mouths. Still it remains a baleful fact that making happiness any sort of an open political demand—or even just a demand of politicians—is a dangerous thing. But at least there was adultery, the current secret code for wanting something *more*. Adultery, whatever its inherent problems—as with other supplements and shopping sprees and pleasure quests—is at least a reliable way of proving to ourselves that we're not in the ground quite yet, especially when feeling a little dead inside. Or at least until a better solution comes along.

The good news from the nation's capital is that hypocrisy doesn't appear to be a sustainable form, no matter how much prophylactic strutting we're subjected to, no matter all the social inducements to practice it regularly. (Consider carefully the advice of right-wing morality czar William Bennett, author of *The Book of Virtues, The Moral Compass,* etc: "Hypocrisy is better than no standards at all.") Hypocrisy may wage a valiant battle against self-recognition, but there's always scandal to trump it. Scandal's desire to make a virtue out of transparency may come with its own set of contradictions, but if its message is that false virtue is the fast track to becoming a national laughingstock, can this be entirely bad?

But what about the well-publicized fears of social conservatives that loose sexual morals undermine existing social institutions? Rather than arguing the point, why not just take our conservative friends at their word: yes, institutional precariousness *is* contagious. The question then, becomes this. If other vows *were* up for examination, if social contracts *could* be renegotiated, what other areas of dissatisfaction would be next on the list? What other paralyzed and sedimented institutions would have to start watching their steps?

Insofar as adultery represents discontent, insofar as it acts on that discontent—even in unformed, inchoate, often temporary ways—insofar as it contains a nascent demand for "something else," does it, as feared, model the possibility of breakouts in other spheres? If the most prohibited sentence for both modern love and modern political life is "Maybe things could be different," does it imperil other fidelity oaths? The Work Harder ethos of our domestic factories, for instance?

Work less, get more!—here's a national motto worth pledging allegiance to.

· · ·

The literature on love is vast. Advice books peddle hard work as the cure-all for faltering desire; all the others ask and answer the same question over and over: "What is love?" No answer appears to suffice, yet still it must be asked, and then asked again. If the definitional quandary stands in for something forever frustrating and forever promising at the core of the whole business, if there's something inherent in the nature of human longing that defeats its own fulfillment—all the while offering fleeting moments of reverie and elusive glimpses of transcendence—then the question is what the social world does with all that frustration and all that promise. Think of the possibilities! Love could be a zone to experiment with wishes and possibilities and even utopian fantasies about gratification and plenitude. Or, love can be harnessed to social utility and come spouting the deadening language of the factory, enfolded in household regimes and quashed desires—an efficient way of organizing acquiescence to shrunken expectations and renunciation and status quos. It can fasten itself to compulsory monogamy—not a desire, but an enforced compliance system. (Which is not to say that monogamy can't be a desire in itself, but you'd really only know that absent the enforcement wing and the security state apparatus.)

Then there's adultery, messing everything up. The practice of dividing the world into categories of clean and polluted, in which what's coded as impure is surrounded by taboos and emotional danger signs, is a cultural universal, anthropologists say. Marriage is our fundamental social structure—"the all-subsuming, all-organizing, all-containing contract," as Tony Tanner puts it—and adultery adulterates it. Clearly the fear is that adultery won't be content to confine its admixing to one household alone; the fear is that it will impinge on all the forms of stability that rest on marital rule-adherence, and the anxiety is palpable in the very semantics of the enterprise. *Adulteration:* note the residues of social purity movements and miscegenation laws, the aura of obsessive handwashing that hovers around the word. Needless to say, anything as fretful as matrimony about maintaining its own purity and its precarious status as the "professedly genuine article" is always going to be especially vulnerable to debasement, no matter how vigilant—

no doubt even attracting debasers for that very reason, like roués to a virgin or your initials to fresh cement. Let's face it: purity always flirts with defilement, shamelessly, just by definition and despite all the protective systems erected in response, privately or socially, from surplus monogamy to "tougher" immigration codes. And what comes of such defensive enterprises but rigid personalities and enervated mono-cultures—or the occasional fascist movement, if you want to be alarmist.

In his essay "Flirtation," the quirky German sociologist Georg Simmel (a contemporary of Freud's) notes that love has a tendency to expire with the fulfillment of its yearning. If love lies on a path from not having to having, Simmel says, invoking Plato, then possessing what you wanted changes the nature of the enterprise—and along with it, the pleasure in it. (Once you have something how can you want it?) Hence the evolution of flirting, a way of being sus-pended between having and not having, and keeping possi-bilities open. Being suspended between consent and refusal is the path to freedom, says Simmel; any decision brings flir-tation to an end. (Simmel's flirts are mostly women, whose spheres of freedom are otherwise socially limited, he reminds us—though these days anyone can play the girl.) Simmel extends his considerations to intellectual flirtation; he's big on flirting with ideas too. Intellectual flirts assert things that aren't really meant in order to test their effect—paradoxes of doubtful authenticity, little threats that aren't seriously intended, false self-disparagements (really they're fishing for compliments); they oscillate between affirming and deny-ing the genuineness of their positions. Simmel happens to find this sort of thing charming. It awakens delight and desire, he effuses, rather making you wonder whom he might have had in mind (or perhaps making you desire to be whom he had in mind)—but then anyone who commits to write an essay on flirtation clearly has a well-honed capacity for sustaining ambiguity.

Maybe no one can be against love, but it's still possible to flirt with the idea. Or, as Adam Phillips asks in his own later essay on the virtues of flirtation, "What does commitment leave out of the picture that we might want?" Note that "against" is one of a few words—like "cleave," another—that can mean both itself and its opposite. It flirts with paradox. (As, perhaps, does anyone who loves.) To cleave is to *split* or *sever;* but to cleave is also to *cling to,* or *remain faithful.* As with "against." To be against means to be *opposed:* resistant or defiant. It also means *next to:* beside or near. Which leaves the problem of a phrase like "up against" which is indeterminate, bivalent—it can play both sides of the street. "Up against love": you would need to know the context to figure out what it means. Or alter the context— here's an idea to flirt with—which could make it mean something else entirely.

SELECTED BIBLIOGRAPHY

A NOTE ON SOURCES

The uses made of innocent books and authors has been frequently speculative and occasionally contrarian: this should probably be regarded as a list of incitations rather than citations in the usual sense. Principal inciters: Chapter 1: Herbert Marcuse, *One-Dimensional Man* (Boston: Beacon Press, 1964); Chapter 2: Michel Foucault, *Discipline and Punish: The Birth of the Prison,* trans. Alan Sheridan (New York: Vintage Books, 1977); Chapter 3: Michel de Certeau, *The Practice of Everyday Life,* trans. Steven Rendall (Berkeley and Los Angeles: University of California Press, 1984), and Peter Bürger, *Theory of the Avant Garde,* trans. Michael Shaw (Minneapolis: University of Minnesota Press, 1984); Chapter 4: Fredric Jameson, *The Political Unconscious: Narrative as a Socially Symbolic Act* (Ithaca, N.Y.: Cornell University Press, 1981).

Inciters—or intellectual dads? But you know how it is with dads: half the time you love them, half the time you want to kill them and eat them. (Or so speculates uber-dad Freud.)

ADDITIONAL SOURCES

Baldick, Chris. *In Frankenstein's Shadow: Myth, Monstrosity, and Nineteenth-Century Writing.* New York: Oxford University Press, 1987.

Barthes, Roland. *A Lover's Discourse: Fragments.* Trans. Richard Howard. New York: Hill and Wang, 1978.

Basch, Norma. *Framing American Divorce: From the Revolu-*

tionary Generation to the Victorians. Berkeley and Los Angeles: University of California Press, 1999.

Berlant, Lauren. *The Queen of America Goes to Washington City: Essays on Sex and Citizenship*. Durham, N.C.: Duke University Press, 1997.

Bloch, Ernst. *The Utopian Function of Art and Literature*. Cambridge, Mass.: MIT Press, 1988.

Bollas, Christopher. *The Shadow of the Object: Psychoanalysis of the Unthought Known*. New York: Columbia University Press, 1987.

Braverman, Harry. *Labor and Monopoly Capital: The Degradation of Work in the Twentieth Century*. New York: Monthly Review Press, 1974.

Chandler, James. *England in 1818: The Politics of Literary Culture and the Case of Romantic Historicism*. Chicago: University of Chicago Press, 1998.

Cott, Nancy. *Public Vows: A History of Marriage and the Nation*. Cambridge, Mass.: Harvard University Press, 2000.

Davis, Lennard. *Enforcing Normalcy: Disability, Deafness, and the Body*. New York: Verso, 1995.

Douglas, Mary. *Purity and Danger: An Analysis of Concepts of Pollution and Taboo*. London: Routledge and Kegan Paul, 1978.

Elias, Norbert. *The History of Manners*. New York: Pantheon Books, 1982.

Engels, Friedrich. *The Origin of the Family, Private Property, and the State*. New York: Pathfinder Press, 1972.

Foucault, Michel. *History of Sexuality. 3 vols*. Trans. Robert Hurley. New York: Pantheon Books, 1978–86.

Freud, Sigmund. *Civilization and Its Discontents*. New York: J. Cape and H. Smith, 1930.

———. "'Civilized' Sexual Morality and Modern Nervous Illness." In *The Standard Edition of the Complete Psychological Works of Sigmund Freud*. Vol. 9. London: Hogarth Press, 1953–74.

———. *Jokes and Their Relation to the Unconscious*. New York: Norton, 1960.

————. "On the Universal Tendency to Debasement in the Sphere of Love." In *The Standard Edition of the Complete Psychological Works of Sigmund Freud.* Vol. 11. London: Hogarth Press, 1953–74.

————. *Three Essays on the Theory of Sexuality.* New York: Basic Books, 2000.

Giddens, Anthony. *The Transformation of Intimacy: Sexuality, Love, and Eroticism in Modern Societies.* Stanford, Calif.: Stanford University Press, 1992.

Ginzburg, Carlo. *The Cheese and the Worms: The Cosmos of a Sixteenth Century Miller.* Trans. John Tedeschi and Anne Tedeschi. New York: Penguin, 1982.

Graff, E. J. *What Is Marriage For? The Strange Social History of Our Most Intimate Institution.* Boston: Beacon Press, 1999.

Gramsci, Antonio. *Prison Notebooks.* 2 vols. Trans. Joseph A. Buttigieg and Antonio Callari. New York: Columbia University Press, 1992–96.

Hariman, Robert. *Political Style: The Artistry of Power.* Chicago: University of Chicago Press, 1995.

Hobsbawm, Eric. *Social Bandits and Primitive Rebels.* New York: Norton, 1959.

Hochschild, Arlie Russell. *The Time Bind: When Work Becomes Home and Home Becomes Work.* New York: Metropolitan Books, 1997.

Iluouz, Eva. *Consuming the Romantic Utopia: Love and the Cultural Contradictions of Capitalism.* Berkeley and Los Angeles: University of California Press, 1997.

Jacoby, Russell. *Social Amnesia: A Critique of Conformist Psychology from Adler to Laing.* Boston: Beacon Press, 1975.

Jameson, Fredric. *The Geopolitical Aesthetic: Cinema and Space in the World System.* Bloomington: Indiana University Press, 1992.

Kernberg, Otto. *Love Relations: Normality and Pathology.* New Haven: Yale University Press, 1995.

Lasch, Christopher. *Haven in a Heartless World: The Family Besieged.* New York: Basic Books, 1977.

Lawson, Annette. *Adultery: An Analysis of Love and Betrayal.* New York: Basic Books, 1988.

Livingston, Judith. "Love and Illusion." *Psychoanalytic Quarterly* 65 (1996).

Marcuse, Herbert. *Eros and Civilization: A Philosophical Inquiry into Freud.* Boston: Beacon Press, 1955.

Marx, Karl. *Capital, A Critique of Political Economy: Volume One.* Trans. Ben Fowkes. New York: Penguin, 1976.

Miller, Gerald R., and James B. Stiff. *Deceptive Communication.* Newbury Park, Calif.: Sage Publications, 1993.

Miller, William Ian. *The Anatomy of Disgust.* Cambridge, Mass.: Harvard University Press, 1997.

Mitchell, Stephen A. *Can Love Last? The Fate of Romance over Time.* New York: Norton, 2002.

Nietzsche, Friedrich. *On the Genealogy of Morals.* Trans. Walter Kaufmann. New York: Vintage Books, 1967.

Pateman, Carole. *The Problem of Political Obligation: A Critical Analysis of Liberal Theory.* Chichester, N.Y.: Wiley, 1979.

Perry, Ruth. "Sleeping With Mr. Collins." *Persuasions* 22 (2000).

Phillips, Adam. *Monogamy.* New York: Vintage Books, 1999.

———. *On Flirtation: Psychoanalytic Essays on the Uncommitted Life.* Cambridge: Harvard University Press, 1994.

Poster, Mark. *Critical Theory of the Family.* New York: Seabury Press, 1978.

Reich, Wilhelm. *Mass Psychology of Fascism.* Trans. Vincent R. Carfagno. New York: Farrar, Straus and Giroux, 1970.

Rougement, Denis de. *Love in the Western World.* Trans. Montgomery Belgion. Princeton, N.J.: Princeton University Press, 1983.

Simmel, Georg. *On Women, Sexuality and Love.* Trans. Guy Oakes. New Haven: Yale University Press, 1984.

Singer, Irving. *The Nature of Love: The Modern World.* Chicago: University of Chicago Press, 1984.

Spurlock, John. *Free Love: Marriage and Middle-Class Radicalism in America, 1825–1860.* New York: New York University Press, 1988.

Stone, Lawrence. *The Family, Sex, and Marriage in England, 1500–1800*. New York: Harper and Row, 1977.

———. "Passionate Attachments in the West in Historical Perspective." In *Passionate Attachments: Thinking about Love*, eds. William Gaylin and Ethel Person. New York: Free Press, 1988.

Tanner, Tony. *Adultery in the Novel: Contract and Transgression*. Baltimore: Johns Hopkins University Press, 1979.

Taylor, Charles. *Sources of the Self: The Making of Modern Identity*. Cambridge: Harvard University Press, 1989.

Thompson, E. P. *The Making of the English Working Class*. New York: Vintage, 1966.

———. "Time, Work-Discipline, and Industrial Capitalism." In *Customs in Common*. London: Merlin Press, and New York: New Press, 1991.

Turner, Victor. "Social Dramas and Stories about Them." *Critical Inquiry* 7, no. 1 (1980).

Warner, Michael. *The Trouble With Normal: Sex, Politics, and the Ethics of Queer Life*. New York: Free Press, 1999.

Weber, Max. *The Protestant Work Ethic and the Spirit of Capitalism*. Trans. Talcott Parsons. New York: Scribner, 1976.

Wexman, Virginia Wright. *Creating the Couple: Love, Marriage, and Hollywood Performance*. Princeton, N.J.: Princeton University Press, 1993.

Zaretsky, Eli. *Capitalism, The Family, and Personal Life*. New York: Harper and Row, 1976.

———. *Secrets of the Soul: Psychoanalysis, Modernity and Personal Life*. New York: Knopf, 2004 (forthcoming).

Zweig, Michael. *The Working Class Majority: America's Best Kept Secret*. Ithaca, N.Y.: ILR Press, 2000.

ABOUT THE AUTHOR

Laura Kipnis teaches at Northwestern University. Her previous books are *Bound and Gagged: Pornography and the Politics of Fantasy in America* and *Ecstasy Unlimited: On Sex, Capital, Gender, and Aesthetics.* She has received fellowships and grants from the Guggenheim Foundation, the Rockefeller Foundation, and the National Endowment for the Arts.